Thank you for purchasing this book!
Because of you, donations will be made that help rescue babies from preventable death and illness.

The death of a baby is always a tragedy. But no mother should ever have to bury her baby when that death could have been prevented! It's heartbreaking to think that 21,000 children under the age of 5 die every day from preventable diseases, most within their first hours or days of life. But here's the good news:

Compassion's Child Survival Program helps developing-world mothers and babies in their most vulnerable times, offering practical care and extending God's love. By joining Kerusso in its effort to Change Lives with Compassion, you're giving them the best chance at life.

Please go to this site to learn how you can do even more in helping moms and babies break the cycle of poverty, compassion.com/kerussocsp.

Compassion International is one of the nation's largest Christian child-sponsorship organizations, working with more than 65 denominations and thousands of indigenous church partners in Africa, Asia, Central and South America, and the Caribbean. Since 1952, Compassion's revolutionary approach, through one-to-one Christian child-sponsorship, has touched the lives of more than 2 million children. **www.compassion.com/kerusso.**

Releasing children from poverty
Compassion®
in Jesus' name

Published in Berryville, Arkansas, by Kerusso. Kerusso is a registered trademark of Kerusso, Inc.

Change your shirt. Change the world! is a registered trademark of Kerusso, Inc.

Scripture quotations marked NIV are taken from the HOLY BIBLE: NEW INTERNATIONAL VERSION®. © 1973, 1978, 1984, 2011 by International Bible Society. Used by permission of Zondervan Publishing House. All rights reserved.

Scripture quotations marked NLT are taken from HOLY BIBLE, NEW LIVING TRANSLATION. © 1996, 2004. Used by permission of Tyndale House Publishers, Inc., Wheaton, Illinois 60189. All rights reserved.

Scripture quotations marked NKJV are taken from THE NEW KING JAMES VERSION. © 1982 by Thomas Nelson, Inc. Used by permission. All rights reserved.

Scripture quotations marked KJV are taken from the King James Version of the Bible. Public domain.

Photography Credits:

Photography courtesy of Thinkstock.com, Vic Kennett, April Lovell, Lorri Carter, Carrie Dan Post, and noelfan.org.

Fireproof and *Courageous* title treatments and images used by arrangement with Sherwood Pictures/Provident Film.

ISBN 978-0-9860128-0-8

Printed in the United States of America
First Edition
10 9 8 7 6 5 4 3 2 1

Dedications

To my Heavenly Father,

Who called me out of darkness into His marvelous light.

To my wife Melody and my children Nikolas, Cassidy, and Kyle,

Your love energizes me every day!

To my Mom and Dad, Margaret and Don Kennett,

Who told me I could accomplish pretty much whatever I put my mind, sweat, and persistence to—and turned out to be right.

To my brothers and sister, Al, Tom, and Cynthia,

Who have all had a hand in my life and success.

To the amazing people of "Team Kerusso",

Who put their hands to the plow with me and made my vision their own.

To my Pastor, Gary Hayhurst,

Who for over 25 years has taught me about my Lord Jesus and our loving Heavenly Father. You've inspired me to reach for all God wants me to be.

I'm forever grateful to you my friend!

ACKNOWLEDGEMENTS

As I say later in this book, there's no such thing as a self-made man - similarly, there's no such thing as an author who produces a book by themself. I am certainly no exception to either of these statements.

My special thanks go out to;

My 25 Artist and Author friends who selflessly lent their names, time, and words to this book's devotions.
Thank you for believing in the cause of T-shirt evangelism!

Meeke Addison, Stephen Baldwin, Joe Bonsall, General Jerry Boykin, Kirk Cameron, Francis Chan, Ray Comfort, Michelle Duggar, Cheri Hamilton, Tim LaHaye, Dennis Lindsay, Alex & Stephen Kendrick, Jane Kirkpatrick, Hal Lindsey, Max Lucado, Josh and Sean McDowell, John Morris, Lauren Nelson and Robin Marsh, Kerri Pomarolli, Jennifer Rothschild, Susie Shellenberger, Wess Stafford, Tammy Trent, Charlie Ward, and J.C. Watts.

My writing and editing team; Jim Fletcher, Lorri Carter, and Jason Anzalone.

To Brent Spurlock for a very creative cover concept!

To the Kerusso and Thinkpen Design teams: Lorri Carter, Jeff Roby, April Lovell, Joe Darby, Markie Qualls, Greg Jackson, and Nathan Pyles - for pulling it all together and making it look amazing!

GOD IS AWESOME!

I HAD GREAT PARENTS. I WAS BLESSED TO GROW UP IN A HOME led by two amazing people who had overcome the Depression, who had built good lives, and who had given back to the community. Honest and hardworking, helpful to their neighbors—Mom and Dad lived this. My parents were really good people. But in this good home, raised by good people, I grew up not knowing God.

We did attend church, but for me church was more about ceremony and ritual. It wasn't "real" to me, and almost nothing about it made a lasting impact on my young heart

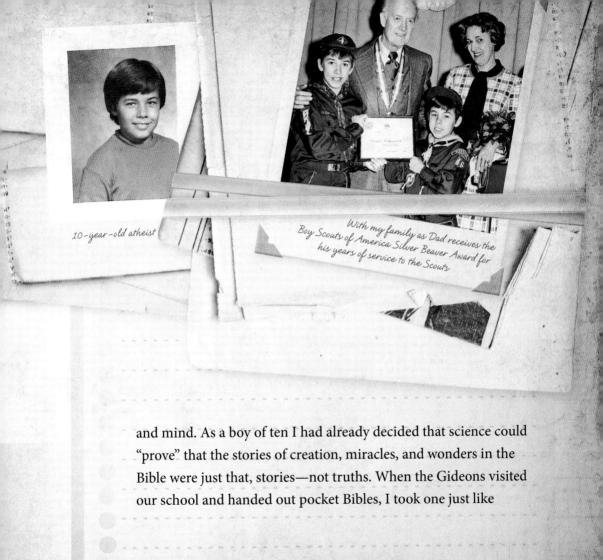

10-year-old atheist

With my family as Dad receives the Boy Scouts of America Silver Beaver Award for his years of service to the Scouts

and mind. As a boy of ten I had already decided that science could "prove" that the stories of creation, miracles, and wonders in the Bible were just that, stories—not truths. When the Gideons visited our school and handed out pocket Bibles, I took one just like

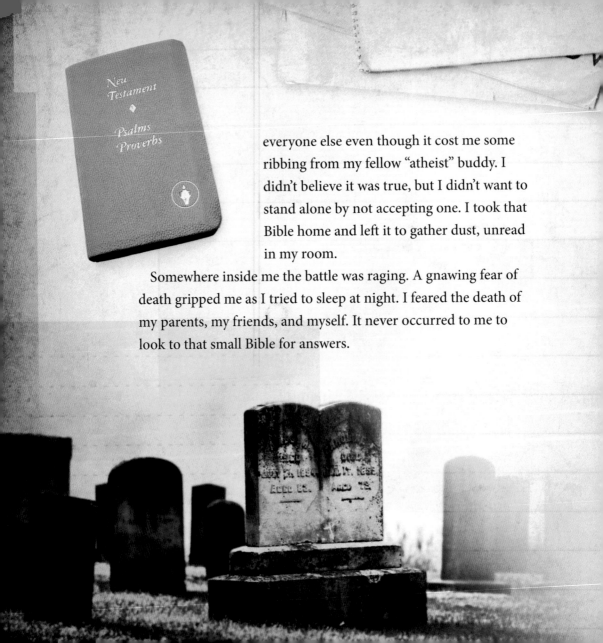

everyone else even though it cost me some ribbing from my fellow "atheist" buddy. I didn't believe it was true, but I didn't want to stand alone by not accepting one. I took that Bible home and left it to gather dust, unread in my room.

Somewhere inside me the battle was raging. A gnawing fear of death gripped me as I tried to sleep at night. I feared the death of my parents, my friends, and myself. It never occurred to me to look to that small Bible for answers.

YARD SALE OF DESTINY

ONE DAY, WHEN I WAS ABOUT FIFTEEN, MY LIFE TOOK AN UNEXPECTED turn. It was an ordinary day, and my mom asked if I wanted to go to a yard sale with her. "A yard sale?" I was busy skateboarding, listening to Boston, and playing Atari on that day. Why would I want to go to a yard sale with my Mom? But I did go. At the sale I looked at all the stuff and picked through the kinds of things you'd normally find at family yard sale—old clothes and shoes, some tools, a plastic flower arrangement, a blender, and a table full of old paperback books. Even though I wasn't much of a reader, the cover of one of those books caught my eye. It was a well-worn copy of Hal Lindsey's *The Late, Great Planet Earth.* I paid a quarter for it and took it home.

I began to read that book, and God used it to begin the process of opening my eyes. Lindsey carefully laid out logical fact-based evidence that the Bible, from Genesis to Revelation, is a trustworthy, historical document. He also brought my attention to the mountain of prophesies contained in it that were fulfilled in the person and life of Jesus of Nazareth. This made me really think about the odds of all these pieces coming together in one person.

"Impossible," I thought—unless there is an all-knowing, all-seeing God who knows the end from the beginning. It is statistically impossible that all the fulfilled prophesies about Jesus, foretold in the Old Testament hundreds of years before He was even born, could be explained as a random series of coincidences! *(continued on page 12)*

I'VE FOUND THAT PEOPLE IN OUR country today don't know much about the Bible. Obviously, then, they don't know much about the amazing Bible prophecies found there.

My own journey to faith in Jesus Christ began when I discovered the so-called "Messianic prophecies," those predictions in the Old Testament that Jesus would come to earth.

There are over 300 of them! I want to focus on only a couple here, but I encourage you to learn more for yourself. You'll be glad you did.

In the tiny book of Micah, we learn about the little, dusty town of Bethlehem located south of Jerusalem. Interestingly, God spoke through the prophets that He planned for the Savior to come from Bethlehem. In just verse 2 alone, we learn three big things:

- *He will be born in a largely unknown town.*
- *He will be a Ruler.*
- *His "origins are from old."*

You need to know that Micah the prophet wrote this 700 years before Jesus was born! If you choose not to believe that, you need to know that the Dead Sea Scrolls, which contain the book of Micah, were copied at least 200 years before the birth of Jesus!

The New Testament record of the fulfillment of His birth is found in Matthew. In Isaiah 9, we learn that Jesus's ministry will begin in Galilee. This was fulfilled, and we see this in the New Testament in Matthew 4:13–15!

These are but two of hundreds of prophecies announcing Jesus Christ, the Hope for the world. I encourage you—urge you—to check these out for yourself.

Continued from page 10

My thinking was changing. If the Bible was a historically accurate and trustworthy text and all these prophesies were true, that obviously pointed to an all-knowing Creator God who knows everything that ever has or will happen. So if there was an all-knowing, all-powerful God and He penned a book (through man) that contained His will for mankind, then I decided I should know what His will was for me.

I learned about God's plan of salvation for mankind and for me personally. I accepted Jesus as my Lord and Savior. **My intellectualized questions faded into knowledge that God loved me and wanted me to live for Him.**

My fears of death evaporated.

I was born again!

Soon I dug out that old Gideon Bible and began to read it. The Word of God opened up a new world to me—a world of absolute truth. One of those truths is found in Mark 16:15. It's a verse that has shaped my life, "He told them, 'Go into all the world and preach the Good News to everyone' " (NLT).

SAVIOR—NOT LORD

LIKE MANY YOUNG BELIEVERS, I WASN'T LIVING OUT MY newfound faith. I wasn't aware of any friends who were living for God that I could fellowship with or going to a church where my faith could be nourished. My heart was changed and my spiritual eyes were open, but the cares of this world and teenage desires were drowning out that still, small voice of the Spirit that was calling me to live a life that pleased God. I hadn't really made Jesus my Lord.

After finishing high school I began attending the UNIVERSITY OF ARKANSAS, where I majored in Business and minored in "partying." I also spent some time on the university's short-lived intercollegiate boxing team, fighting in the middleweight division. After a few years I lost sight of the value of a higher education. My enthusiasm and my grades were really low, so I dropped out of school and into business.

I credit **my dad** for instilling **a strong work ethic** and **"can do"** attitude in me from a very young age. He told me that I could pretty much **accomplish whatever** I put my mind and efforts to. Dad taught me the values of **hard work**, paying my own way, **saving my money**, keeping my word, and a lot of other things that have served me well in my life. I started working at my uncle's motel when I was just twelve years old. From age twelve on, I always had at least one summer job and usually two. In addition to the various day jobs I had over the summers, at night I was a cast member of the Great Passion Play in Eureka Springs Arkansas, where I lived.

Vic's Dad, Don Kennett

AFTER LEAVING THE COLLEGE LIFE,
I decided to open a fitness center.
Fitness and bodybuilding were
passions of mine and something I did
and read a lot about, so I thought it
was a natural thing for me. I was only
twenty years old when I opened *Fit
for Life Fitness and Racquet Club* using
up all the money I'd saved from my
summer jobs over the years. I worked
a ton of hours and was open seven
days a week.

FIT FOR LIFE
family health club
and racquetball

FIT FOR LIFE 09-84
FAMILY HEALTH CLUB AND RACQUETBALL
1 VAN BUREN PH. 501-253-8578
EUREKA SPRINGS, AR 72632

FIT FOR LIFE
family health club
and racquetball

PAY
TO THE
ORDER OF

*Newlyweds Vic and Melody
at Fit for Life.*

Bank
of EUREKA
SPRINGS
EUREKA SPRINGS, AR 72632

VOID = 2
APR 17 1985

FOR

⑈000 70 ⑈ ⑈:08 29 ⑈: 0008⑈30 2⑈2⑈

One Sunday morning I was watching a TV preacher. In my wandering years, pretty much ever since I'd accepted Jesus as Savior, I was always aware of God being with me and in me, even if I wasn't being obedient to Him. But that Sunday morning God really got my attention. Although it wasn't an audible voice, it was a very clear voice that said, *"You've said you're a Christian all these years; it's time to start living like one."* I thank God for His wake-up call that day in the spring of 1985. I've never regretted saying "Yes, Father, I will."

I went broke in the fitness business after only a couple years; our small community just couldn't support it. After that I had a couple of different sales jobs but finally settled into working as a carpenter—how ironic!

I liked building things—always have—but I wasn't content with my work path and felt God moving in me to pursue something else. As I worked I would think about that verse from Mark 16 and think about ways that I could use my life to "Go into all the world." I'm no writer or preacher and didn't think I was called to a foreign mission field—I needed to find something that suited my skills and interests. One of the summer jobs I held as a teenager from ages 15–19 was store manager of a small T-shirt shop.... the kind you might find in a resort town where you pick out a "transfer" and they press it on to a T-shirt with a heat press. So I guess you could say I had a little bit of a T-shirt background and always paid attention to them.

One day, as I was on my hands and knees scraping up old tile during a renovation of public restrooms, I saw a tourist wearing a T-shirt with a Christian message on it. I don't remember what it said, but I remember thinking, "Wow, that's really cool—that's what I want to do!" Later I looked again to that verse in Mark and learned that the Greek word for preach was *kerusso*: *Jesus said unto them, "go into all the world and* **'kerusso'** *the Good News to everyone."*

And that's how Kerusso was born. I began a journey filled with testing and triumph—always leaning on Jesus, the Carpenter from Nazareth.

Jesus said,

"Go into all the world and

'kērussō'

the Good News to everyone."

("kērussō" is the Greek word for preach)

DO YOU "*kērussō*"?

DUMPSTER-DIVING FOR JESUS

WITH THE VISION FOR KERUSSO NOW IN HAND, IT WAS TIME TO get to work! Still stinging from the failure and financial loss of Fit for Life, I vowed that I wouldn't take on any "real" debt to get the new business going. Flat-broke and living meager paycheck to paycheck, I borrowed $1,000 in seed money from my brother Al.

Al and Vic

I developed a few designs and decided to sell them directly to consumers through small ads in *Campus Life* magazine. I'm sure some of you remember those days before the Internet when you actually had to mail in a check or money order to an address and wait 3–6 weeks for your merchandise. Well, that was the process in our early days. Someone had to see our little 1/6th of a page black-and-white ad (color ads were too expensive for our start-up), fill out the tiny order form, and mail us a check. Still working in construction at the time, I would go to the post office on my lunch break and check the mailbox to see if I had any orders. In the orders came! Just a handful at a time, not much—but pretty exciting for our fledgling company. I saved up the orders until I had enough to meet the minimum-order requirements of our local screen printer. Then, at night, when my day job was over, I would pack them up and ship them out. Not able to afford the luxury of buying shipping boxes, I would go dumpster-diving at the local drugstore and hardware stores. I'm sure many of my customers had some puzzling experiences.

"Martha, did you order a box of baby food and nails?!"

Orders were coming in pretty well from the first few ads, but after that things slowed to a trickle. With just a few orders in hand, not enough for the minimum print runs, I considered throwing in the towel. But my sister Cynthia (God bless her!) gave me a pep talk and said, "Just hang in there and give God a chance to make it work." And that's what I did! Right after that God led me to go out and try selling our T-shirts wholesale to some local Christian book and gift stores. I took a day off from construction and visited several local stores within a 60-mile radius. With a few samples and one of my wife's waitress pads in hand, I was actually able to write some orders! Kerusso was saved and I was able to fulfill that handful of consumer orders. Praise God!

With the new approach of selling to retail stores in play, I was off and running!

The orders became consistent enough that I decided to start printing my own shirts. With a small press and some homemade dryers I set up shop in a spare bedroom of our home. Basically self-taught, I printed thousands of shirts by hand with that equipment. My mom would come by and help fold the shirts from time to time so I could keep printing, selling, and shipping.

My wife Melody was the real breadwinner in those days, so she wasn't able to join in on all the fun.

Vic's Mom and first "employee"

Judah St. — Kerusso's first home

I found a small sales rep group who specialized in the Christian retail market. They took on Kerusso as one of their lines and represented us in about six states. To help them market our shirts, I took on the task of making brochures. I did my own product photography and pasted up a one-page brochure that was printed by our local printer.

Eventually a larger rep group that covered all fifty states approached me, and they went to work selling Kerusso nationwide.

After that I was too busy with Kerusso to keep my job as a carpenter, and I hung up the hammer for good.

My last carpentry project before going full time on Kerusso—A floating gazebo on Lake Lucerne near Eureka Springs, Ar.

Soon we outgrew the print shop at home and moved into half of a small metal building next to a car-repair service. Our new space seemed cavernous compared to the space we started in.

Before long we would need every inch of that spacious 1,500 square feet to set Kerusso on the path to long-term success. We doubled our space when the other half of that building became available, and we doubled again a few years after that when we built our own building in nearby Berryville, where Kerusso is located today. Since then we've added on many more times to that original 6,000-square-foot building and purchased two surrounding properties. Today Kerusso fills over 60,000 square feet of warehouse, production, and office space in three buildings sitting on our 10-acre campus. God has brought us to this place, and He has allowed us to come here debt-free. God is so good!

NO SUCH THING AS A "SELF-MADE" MAN

Owning my own company has taught me so much. I've had to learn every aspect of business. From designing and product development, sales and marketing, to operations, finance, and human resources management, I've gained an incredible education.

Looking back at it now, it's amazing to me that Kerusso survived those early years. I really didn't know what I was doing, but God was faithful as I did my best to serve Him.

I don't pull the squeegee in production or move the mouse in graphic design anymore, but I'm still very hands-on in the development of every single product we make and in running the company. God has blessed me beyond measure, and this journey would have been impossible in my own strength.

Today the Kerusso family has grown to over one hundred team members who are passionate about what we do. It's their dedication, passion, and hard work, along with the grace of God, that continues to make us a success. It really is true that God is able to do exceedingly abundantly above all that we ask or even think!

Kerusso®
Proclaiming the Good News to the world, through products about Jesus.
TEAM KERUSSO

Kerusso has shared the gospel on every continent and in over 100 countries.

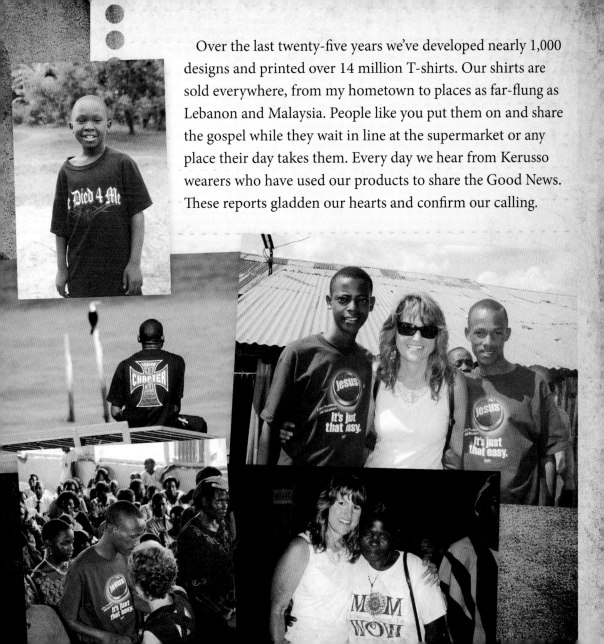

Over the last twenty-five years we've developed nearly 1,000 designs and printed over 14 million T-shirts. Our shirts are sold everywhere, from my hometown to places as far-flung as Lebanon and Malaysia. People like you put them on and share the gospel while they wait in line at the supermarket or any place their day takes them. Every day we hear from Kerusso wearers who have used our products to share the Good News. These reports gladden our hearts and confirm our calling.

Sharing the Good News of Jesus Christ is what Kerusso has been about from the start. "Proclaiming the Good News to the World, through Products about Jesus" is our company's mission statement and why we exist. We use our products to tell the world that there is a God who loves them and wants a relationship with them and that Jesus is the only way. We have shared this story on every continent and in over one hundred countries.

I thank God He reached out to me and put *The Late, Great Planet Earth* in front of me when I was a teenager.

I thank Him for imparting the vision for Kerusso in my early twenties.

I thank Him for all the wonderful people He sent to join us over these twenty-five years.

I'm grateful for all the retailers who carry our products to the world, and I thank God for every believer who decides to change their shirt and change the world!

Vic Kennett—today, standing where the vision for Kerusso was imparted—holding what's left of one of their first t-shirts.

HE DID THIS JUST FOR YOU

This T-shirt was produced
from 2001 to 2006

*Used with permission
from *He Did This Just for You*;
Thomas Nelson Publishers;
February 2005.

THE WAY HOME

BY MAX LUCADO

The most notorious road in the world is the Via Dolorosa, "the Way of Sorrows." According to tradition, it is the route Jesus took from Pilate's hall to Calvary. The path is marked by stations frequently used by Christians for their devotions. One station marks the passing of Pilate's verdict. Another, the appearance of Simon to carry the cross. Two stations commemorate the stumble of Christ; another the words of Christ. There are fourteen stations in all, each one a reminder of the events of Christ's final journey.

Is the route accurate? Probably not. When Jerusalem was destroyed in A.D. 70 and again in A.D. 135, the streets of the city were destroyed. As a result, no one knows the exact route Christ followed that Friday.

But we do know where the path actually began.

The path began not in the court of Pilate, but in the halls of heaven. The Father began his journey when he left home in search of us. Armed with nothing more than a passion to win your heart, he came looking.

This is the heart of the Christian message. God became human. He was born in an ordinary stable to ordinary parents, but his was an extraordinary purpose. He came to take us to heaven. His death was a sacrifice for our sins. Jesus was our substitute. He paid for our mistakes so we wouldn't have to. Jesus's desire was singular—to bring his children home. The Bible has a word for this quest: *reconciliation.*

"God was in Christ reconciling the world to Himself" (2 Corinthians 5:19 NKJV). The Greek word for *reconcile* means "to render something otherwise." The path to the cross tells us exactly how far God will go to put it back together. Reconciliation restitches the unraveled, reverses the rebellion, rekindles the cold passion.

Reconciliation touches the shoulder of the wayward and woos him homeward.

MAX LUCADO loves words—written, spoken, it does not matter. He loves to craft sentences that are memorable, inspiring, and hopefully life-changing. In almost 25 years of writing, more than 100 million products—80 million books—filled with his words have been sold. Lucado is a Minister of Preaching at Oak Hills Church in San Antonio, where he has served since 1988, and he is currently serving as a contributing editor for *Leadership Journal* magazine. He has been married to Denalyn Preston Lucado since 1981, and they have three grown daughters—Jenna, Andrea, and Sara—and one son-in-law, Brett.

GOD LOVED THE WORLD
SO MUCH THAT **HE**
GAVE HIS ONE AND ONLY
SON SO THAT WHOEVER
BELIEVES
IN HIM MAY NOT BE LOST,
BUT HAVE ETERNAL
LIFE.

IN CHRIST I AM...

DELIVERED
ALIVE
SALT &
FREE

GOD'S WORKMANSHIP
SEALED
HOLY
HEALED
INHERITOR
CHILD FORTUNATE
FREE
JOYFUL
CHAMPION
TRIUMPHANT
SIGNIFICANT
BLESSED

FIRMLY ROOTED
SET FREE
ANOINTED COMPLETE
HEIR
SECURE
SAVED

COMPLETE
NEW FOLLOWER
NEW CREATURE
SUCCESSFUL
PRIVILEGED
WARRIOR
LOVED
JOINT-HEIR

CONQUEROR
ASSURED
NEW
ALIVE
BELOVED
STRONG
RECONCILED
EXONERATED
ESTABLISHED
SANCTIFIED

FORGIVEN

UNSHACKLED
FAVORED
IMPROVED
CONFIDENT

UNCHAINED

DEAD
TO SIN
TRANSFORMED
OVERCOMER
LABORER
DEVOTED
LOVED
FREE
CHOSEN
NEW
MINISTER
ALIVE
ABSOLVED
JUSTIFIED
PARDONED
PROTECTED
UNCHAINED

BELIEVER
WITNESS
ACCEPTED
HEIR
ALIVE
IN CHRIST
EXEMPT
RECONCILED

Colossians 2:10
When you have
Christ, you are
complete.

This T-shirt was
introduced in 2012.

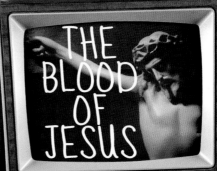

In Christ I Am

Everywhere you look there it is...the world telling you where your self worth comes from. The message being sent through the media, movie stars, and magazines is that your self-worth comes from "what you have," "what you do," and "what you look like." Fame, fortune, and beauty can quickly turn into an obsession of trying to measure up. And if you find yourself in the trap of trying to identify yourself by these human standards, you will always fall short because the world's message is always changing.

Looking to outward things to define our worth only leads to hurt and heartache.

Why not look to God, who made you, and believe what His Word says about having an identity in Christ? Do you know that God loves you so much He sent Jesus to die so you could know Him personally? When you trust Christ, it is a life-changing experience. Christ changes your life by all that He offers you. Not only is it security in the promise of the life to come in heaven...but it is also a promise of abundant life for the here and now. God's Word, the Bible, shares about who we are in Christ. If you are a believer, think about what it truly means to have an identity "in Christ." You are delivered, chosen, set free, loved, forgiven, blessed, sealed, and alive. You are also unshackled, favored, transformed, protected, complete, joyful, and so much more. And you have the promise that a relationship with Christ means that He will always be with you. When you face a tough time, He is there. He will never leave you.

Quit weighing yourself on the world's scales that only lead to an identity crisis. Remember that you are a child of God. Walk in the truth that He loves you and has given you more blessings than this world can ever afford.

WHO ARE YOU IN CHRIST?

Loved
Adored
Beautiful
chosen
free
forgiven

...N MARSH is a national award-
...ng journalist with almost 30 years
...ience in broadcast news. She
...ors the weekday morning news
...TV in Oklahoma City, Oklahoma.
...uses her influence from television
...ay to share with women and girls
...e of Jesus at retreats for women,
...ts, and churches.

LAUREN NELSON was crowned
Miss America 2007. She received the
prestigious TOYA award (Ten Outstanding
Young Americans) by the United
States Junior Chamber organization
in 2008. Lauren is a coanchor at KWTV
in Oklahoma City, Oklahoma. Lauren
loves teaching Bible studies and leading
worship with her husband.

Be a Social Hazard!

BY STEPHEN BALDWIN

A "hazard"—that's kind of an ugly image, an image that most don't strive for, and that's especially true for a person like me who came up in the entertainment world. Actors, at least ones who want to advance their careers, might opt for edgy, gritty roles, but the public persona is usually about conforming to the culture around us.

That's not for me. At least not anymore.

MY LIFE BEFORE CHRIST WAS DAY-TO-DAY SELF-ABSORBANCE. IT WAS ABOUT THE PURSUIT OF MONEY.

Today, loving Jesus is the most important thing to me. I know it sounds hokey...but it's the truth.

Let me tell you how I became a social hazard, determined to knock over the devil's designs for lost and hurting people.

Back in the '90s, my wife and I were living in Tucson, and we hired a cleaning lady. She would sing, and one day my wife approached her and said, "Why is it that every song you sing is about Jesus?"

SOCIAL

I WILL NOT
CONFORM
TO THE

PATTERN
OF THIS
WORLD

ROMANS
12:2

WARNING!

HAZARD

This T-shirt was
introduced in 2012

Agusta burst out laughing and said, "The reason I'm laughing is because you think the only reason I'm here is to clean your house!" She went on to tell my wife that in the future, she and I were to become born-again Christians and have a ministry.

Really?

At the time, I was making more money in my career than I'd ever dreamed about. But as I got to a place where I could say "I believe Jesus is the Son of God," real change began to take place in me.

I was no longer striving to conform to the world, but I began to see that there was another side to the "edgy, gritty" coin, and that I could in fact put myself out there as an example of a changed life through Christ. I did not mind becoming "socially unacceptable" in the community of my peers.

My book, *The Unusual Suspect*, and ministry endeavors like Breakthrough Ministry, which incorporates extreme sports, have taken me to places I never thought about in my old life.

I'M SO GLAD TO BE ABLE TO SAY THAT WAS MY OLD LIFE, AS I AM A NEW CREATURE IN CHRIST!

How about you? Are you too concerned about what people think about you and your walk of faith, are you conforming to the ways of this world, or are you boldly standing as a witness for Jesus? Don't "Fit In" to this world—be a social hazard to it!

A member of one of America's leading acting families, **STEPHEN BALDWIN** has starred in such films as *The Usual Suspects, Fled, Born on the Fourth of July,* and *The Flyboys*. His television work includes a turn as Buffalo Bill Cody in *The Young Riders*.

Raised Catholic, Baldwin's embrace of evangelical Christianity gained the notice of the wider culture, and his work in evangelism now dominates his life both professionally and privately. Baldwin has cofounded ministries, including **The AsSalt Tour**, which incorporates the use of extreme sports in evangelism efforts. Stephen is also passionately involved with **I am second.com.** and **Food for Orphans.org.** The 2006 release of his book, *The Unusual Suspect*, established him as a major figure in evangelical circles; he currently lives in New York with his wife and two children.

FISHERS OF MEN

SINCE
A.D. 33

You catch 'em   God cleans 'em

"FOLLOW ME AND I WILL MAKE YOU FISHERS OF MEN"
MATTHEW 4:19

This T-shirt was
introduced in 2009

Fishers of Men!

By Dennis Lindsay

When my parents, Gordon and Freda Lindsay, started Christ for the Nations (CFN) in 1948, it was simply another step along the road of evangelism they had been on for many years. My parents' greatest desire was to see the lost won to Jesus Christ! They didn't have a fishing show on television, but, boy, were they "fishers"!

They understood a key point about evangelism: we each have a mandate from the Lord Jesus Himself to tell people the wonderful Good News…but it is solely the Lord's work to "clean the catch." Our mission is simple. This concept is so simple to grasp, it should encourage each of us to practice evangelism wherever our journey takes us. God Himself told the apostles—men who made their living in the fishing industry of their day—that all believers can be fishermen but in a spiritual sense.

My parents were impacted from an early age by the Bible stories of the apostles taking the Gospel to the lost. In particular, they identified with Peter, the lowly fisherman whose ministry eventually went far beyond the Galilee. The single-minded purpose of winning souls to Jesus Christ kept my parents in a place of humbleness that enabled CFN to flower. Part of our "ten-point" priority list that we continually emphasize at CFN is "Water Walker," or people of faith. I am always captivated by that image, especially of course when I visit the Sea of Galilee in the land I love. Believe me, my life's work is wrapped up in pulling in those nets of new believers!

When Matthew recorded Jesus's command to "follow me," he understood the spiritual corollary of this message to a handful of Galilean fishermen. That's why He selected the "common people"—to alert the rest of us that evangelizing

the world is not reserved for the most intelligent, gifted "fishers." We are all invited to toss a line into the ocean of humanity and see lives changed for eternity.

If we keep in mind at all times that our Lord has given us a great and wonderful task in sharing His message of redemption with individuals and that we don't have the added pressure of trying to make whole the person's "flopping, wiggling, slippery, messed-up life," well, there is joy in that.

DENNIS LINDSAY is president and CEO of Christ for the Nations (CFN), in Dallas, Texas. CFN was founded by his parents, Gordon and Freda Lindsay, in 1948, and during the past 63 years has helped complete over 12,400 church buildings worldwide, provided over 60 million pieces of free Christian teaching literature in 80 languages, and trained over 30,000 students at their Institute. Like his parents, Dennis and his wife, Ginger, carry on the work at CFN as a team, together with a remarkable family of volunteers and staff.

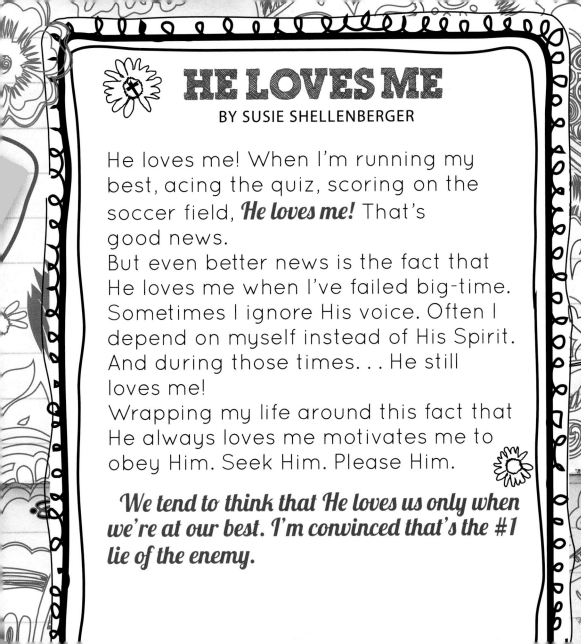

HE LOVES ME

BY SUSIE SHELLENBERGER

He loves me! When I'm running my best, acing the quiz, scoring on the soccer field, *He loves me!* That's good news.

But even better news is the fact that He loves me when I've failed big-time. Sometimes I ignore His voice. Often I depend on myself instead of His Spirit. And during those times. . . He still loves me!

Wrapping my life around this fact that He always loves me motivates me to obey Him. Seek Him. Please Him.

We tend to think that He loves us only when we're at our best. I'm convinced that's the #1 lie of the enemy.

The Bible shows me that His love for us is totally about the cross and what was accomplished there—not about our performance.

He loves me. He loves me. He truly loves me! How do I know? Because Isaiah 49:16 tells me that He loves me so much, He has engraved me in the palms of His hands.

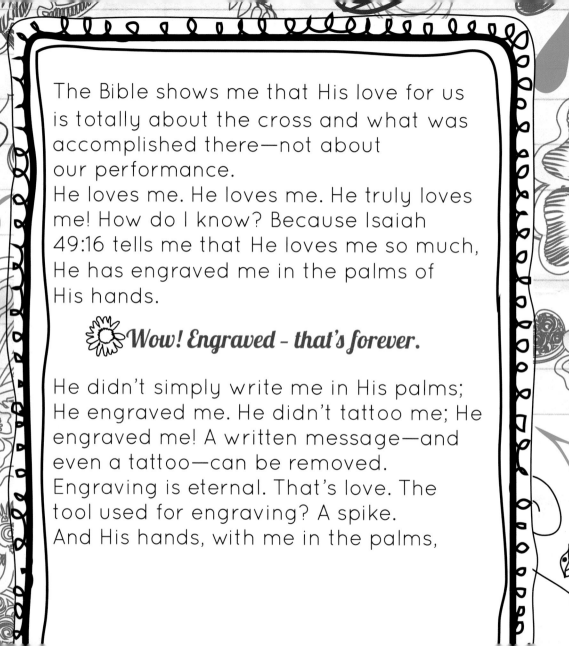 *Wow! Engraved - that's forever.*

He didn't simply write me in His palms; He engraved me. He didn't tattoo me; He engraved me! A written message—and even a tattoo—can be removed. Engraving is eternal. That's love. The tool used for engraving? A spike. And His hands, with me in the palms, were then attached to an ugly cross. He died with me in His hands. I can't ignore a love like that. I serve a risen Savior who loves me. When I'm at the top of my game. . . and when I'm at my worst. And the best part?

Nothing – absolutely nothing – can separate me from His love.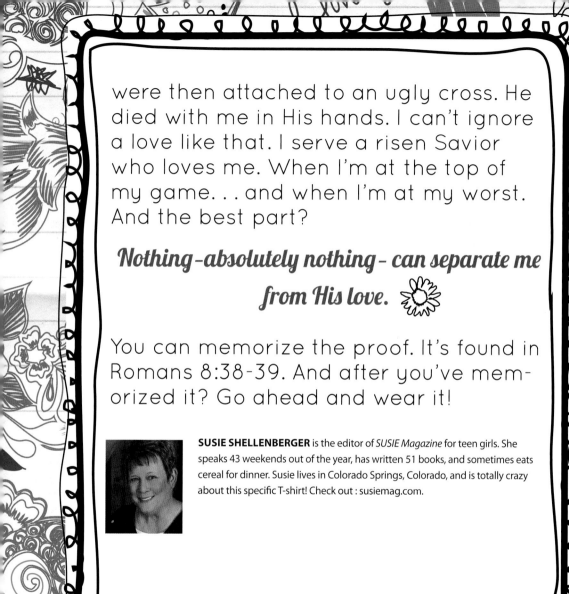

You can memorize the proof. It's found in Romans 8:38-39. And after you've memorized it? Go ahead and wear it!

SUSIE SHELLENBERGER is the editor of *SUSIE Magazine* for teen girls. She speaks 43 weekends out of the year, has written 51 books, and sometimes eats cereal for dinner. Susie lives in Colorado Springs, Colorado, and is totally crazy about this specific T-shirt! Check out : susiemag.com.

GIVE IT ALL YOU GOT.

PLAY TO WIN - LIVE FOR CHRIST

AND GIVE ALL THE GLORY TO GOD

PLAY TO WIN - LIVE FOR CHRIST

"Be exalted, O God, above the heavens, and let your glory be over all the earth." Psalm 108:5

This T-shirt was produced from 2004 to 2007.

ATHLETE IN ACTION

By Charlie Ward

They say the odds of lightning striking the same place twice are very slim. An athlete finding himself or herself on a championship team can be just as slim. But that doesn't mean it can't happen. It happened to me!

Being part of a championship team requires a great attitude.

Our attitude plays a big part in life. If we don't have a positive attitude, we won't get anywhere. I have always tried to maintain a positive attitude, and it has served me well in athletics. Above all, my attitude comes from my relationship with Jesus Christ.

He is the real Ultimate Champion.

There are opportunities to make an impact for the Ultimate Champion when you are on His winning team.

All this puts life into perspective. For example, "I" won the Heisman Trophy at Florida State University my senior year, in 1993. Yet without an all-world offensive line and great receivers and backs, I would have been flat on my back every play. Jesus didn't even boast of Himself, but rather He boasted of His Father in heaven.

That's our goal, to not boast about ourselves.

The Lord blessed me with athletic skills, and I have used them only for one real reason: I get an opportunity to influence young people on a daily basis. After my professional basketball career, I began coaching young people and today am the head football coach at Westbury Christian School in Houston. It is here that we learn what it means to be a true champion.

At Florida State, the team won a national football championship my senior year; it remains a wonderful memory. Yet while the rings and trophies are nice, winning at life is a much bigger prize, and I am happy to tell anyone and everyone that Jesus Christ is the key to that.

In my current role, there are enormous opportunities to build individual champions. The main goal is to share Christ with kids and to mold young people's minds. There are a lot of teach-able moments!

You too can be on a championship team, and with Him there are no slim odds. You win every time with Christ!

Charlie Ward played for four years as quarterback for the Florida State Seminoles, where he won the Heisman Trophy. He then spent 11 years in the NBA as a point guard, most of that time with the New York Knicks. He is an outspoken ambassador for Christ and the head football coach at Westbury Christian School in Houston.

Photos of Charlie Ward at Florida State and with the Knicks courtesy of www.nolefan.org.

Jesus

THE LION OF JUDAH
REVELATION 5:5

This T-shirt was produced from 2005 to 2009.

The Lion of Judah

Revelation 5:5 reveals Him to be Jesus Christ, and when He returns physically to this earth one day, to rescue it from destruction, He will rule and reign forever.

THE LION OF JUDAH

CHRIST IN PROPHECY
BY HAL LINDSEY

The study of Bible prophecy is not really so complex, although some try to make it that way. Actually, it is joy, because through predictive prophecy we find our true peace, in the Person of Jesus Christ.

Because all of Scripture points to Jesus, and because about a third of the Bible deals with prophecy, it is key in developing a worldview that leads us to faith in Christ—He our Redeemer and substitute for the penalty of sin.

Like many people, I held various jobs before settling into my life's calling of an evangelist and writer. I was even a tugboat captain for a time! But my study of prophecy, and the hundreds of Messianic prophecies in the Old Testament, compelled me to study at Dallas Theological Seminary.

HAL LINDSEY Hal Lindsey is an internationally acclaimed writer and speaker with more than a dozen books to his name, including best seller and perennial classic *The Late, Great Planet Earth*. Dr. Lindsey is host of *The Hal Lindsey Report* www.hallindsey.com.

I discovered a fascinating description in Scripture, that of the "Lion of Judah." In Revelation 5:5, we read of the "Lion of the tribe of Judah." Judah of course was the son of Jacob (later renamed "Israel" by the Lord), and would become father of one of the famed Twelve Tribes of Israel.

I mentioned those Messianic prophecies before, those passages that tell us who the Redeemer would be. Revelation 5:5 reveals Him to be Jesus Christ, and when He returns physically to this earth one day, to rescue it from destruction, He will rule and reign forever. The lion has come to symbolize strength and regal character in our culture and has been known affectionately over the years as the "king of the jungle."

The Ultimate King is coming one day soon—make sure you know Him!

This is the day the LORD has made: LET US REJOICE AND BE GLAD IN IT! PSALM 118:24

This T-shirt was introduced in 2011.

CHOOSE JOY

BY: MICHELLE DUGGAR

As a wife and mom, my heart's desire is to share with moms who have young children. There's a certain season of life we come to that seems much more trying than other seasons.

And for me, when I had six children under the age of six and was expecting my seventh baby, I remember just feeling very overwhelmed. It was a probably a crisis of faith that I'd come to at that time. I remember one night I was standing in the laundry room, late. Crying out to my Lord, with tears streaming down my cheeks, and I remember saying to my Father, "Surely, Lord, you've picked the wrong person for this job. I feel so overwhelmed and so inadequate."

I remember a still, small voice: "Michelle, I'm here. Are you willing to praise Me, even when it's hard, when things are not easy?"

I just lifted up my hands and began to praise the Lord and sang, "The Joy of the Lord Is My Strength!" It was a sacrifice, because at that moment I didn't feel like it.

It was amazing. A real burden lifted off my shoulders!

Nothing changed overnight. I had just as much laundry to do. But there was such a peace that came over me.

Later, I went to piano lessons with my children. The piano teacher noticed that I was always nodding off to sleep. She said, "Michelle, are you okay?"

I told her I stayed home at night doing laundry, and she said, "Laundry? I love to do laundry! I'd be happy to come and help you do laundry."

My mouth just about dropped open to the floor!

That Saturday she came to my home, and several hours later I had baskets of fresh, clean clothes.

That was 13 years ago.

I share all that because we all go through different struggles in our lives, and many come to a place in life that is a crisis of faith. What are we going to do then? Through this, I realized God was saying to me, "Michelle, you have to choose joy. Despite what you feel, choose joy."

"Despite what you feel, choose joy."

That incident with the laundry always reminds me of my life verse, 2 Corinthians 12:9, where we are told that our Lord's grace is sufficient for us. It helps to keep Jesus the central focus of life!

MICHELLE DUGGAR lives with her husband, Jim Bob, and their 19 children in northwest Arkansas, and their lives are chronicled on the TLC program, *19 Kids & Counting*. Michelle is the author or coauthor of several books, including *A Love That Multiplies*. Find out more about Michelle and the Duggars at www.duggarfamily.com.

GOD IS LOVE

(Crazy, Relentless, All-Powerful Love)

HOLDING NOTHING BACK

By Francis Chan

After the apostle Peter preached on the day of Pentecost, people "were cut to the heart and said…'Brothers, what shall we do?'" (Acts 2:37 NIV). The first church responded with immediate action: repentance, baptism, selling possessions, sharing the gospel.…

We say things like, "I can do all things through Christ who strengthens me," and "Trust in the Lord with all your heart." Then we live and plan like we don't believe God even exists. We try to set up our lives so everything will be fine even if God doesn't come through. **BUT TRUE FAITH MEANS HOLDING NOTHING BACK.** It means putting every hope in God's fidelity to His promises. A friend of mine once said that Christians are like manure: spread them out and they help everything grow better, but keep them in one big pile and they stink horribly. Which are you? The kind that reeks, around which people walk a wide swath? Or the kind that trusts God enough to let Him spread you out—whether that means going outside your normal group of Christian friends, increasing your material giving, or using your time to serve others?

I was convicted by my lack of faith in college. I realized that my choices had situated me in a pile of stinking manure, and this motivated me to put myself in uncomfortable situations. I began going into downtown Los Angeles to share my faith. I didn't "hear God calling me" to drive downtown; I just chose to go. I obeyed. Most of us use "I'm waiting for God to reveal His calling on my life" as a means of avoiding action. Did you hear God calling you to sit in front of the television yesterday? Or to go on your last vacation? Or to exercise this morning? Probably not, but you still did it. The point isn't that vacations or exercise are wrong, but that we are quick to rationalize our entertainment and priorities yet slow to commit to serving God.…

JESUS SAID, "IF YOU LOVE ME, YOU WILL OBEY WHAT I COMMAND" [JOHN 14:15 NIV 1984]. Jesus did not say, "If you love me, you will obey me when you feel called or good about doing so.…" If we love, then we obey. Period. This sort of matter-of-fact obedience is part of what it means to live a life of faith.

The greatest blessing I received during those trips to the inner city was seeing God work in situations where He has to. As a result, I've made a commitment to consistently put myself in situations that scare me and require God to come through. When I survey my life, I realize that those times have been the most meaningful and satisfying of my life. They were the times when I truly experi-

GOD IS CALLING YOU
TO A PASSIONATE LOVE RELATIONSHIP WITH HIMSELF.
BECAUSE THE ANSWER TO RELIGIOUS COMPLACENCY
ISN`T WORKING HARDER
AT A LIST OF DOS AND DON`TS-
IT`S FALLING IN LOVE WITH GOD.

Read Matthew 22:37-40

crazy love

FRANCIS CHAN is the best-selling author of books *Crazy Love, Forgotten God,* and *Erasing Hell* and the host of the*BASIC.series (Who is God and We Are Church)*. He has also written the children's books *Halfway Herbert, The Big Red Tractor and the Little Village,* and *Ronnie Wilson's Gift.*

Francis is the founding pastor of Cornerstone Church in Simi Valley, California, and is the founder of Eternity Bible College. He also sits on the board of directors of the Children's Hunger Fund and World Impact.

Currently, Francis is working to start a church-planting movement in the inner city of San Francisco as well as launching a countrywide discipleshiping movement. Francis now lives in Northern California with his wife, Lisa, and their five children.

T-SHIRT EVANGELISM

IN 1955 JAMES DEAN WORE A SIMPLE WHITE T-SHIRT IN THE landmark film *Rebel without a Cause*. Almost overnight the sales of this staple piece of men's underwear went through the roof—the T-shirt which had, up to this time, been strictly an undergarment had now became a symbol of individuality. All the cool cats and those who aspired to be cool wore them. By the 1960s a cottage industry selling airbrushed tees had sprung up at hot-rod shows, and by the end of the decade the technology had been developed to mass-produce screen-printed tees. From the very beginning, printed tees have been a way for us to make a statement about all kinds of things—humor, politics, beer, revolution, movies, stars, cars, kittens, and yes, even Jesus. If it matters to you, you want to wear it on a T-shirt. They have become a staple of our wardrobes that let us express ourselves without saying a word. I don't care if you are two or ninety-two, you probably have a few in your drawer, and they are likely to be some your favorite things to wear.

When we wear printed T-shirts we are expressing ourselves, we want to be heard…but are we saying anything that really matters? Did you know that a graphic tee will be read as many as three thousand times

in its lifetime before heading to the rag box!? A printed T-shirt turns us into effective walking billboards, marketers of whatever we are wearing on our T-shirts. Is wearing a "*Just Do It*" shirt going to make a difference in the world—or just help Nike sell more sneakers? Now, don't get me wrong, I like Nike! I'm not saying you should feel badly if you don't wear a witnessing T-shirt all the time! I'm saying, why not use the opportunity to make a statement about something that really DOES matter? Why not say something that can change a person's life for all eternity?

WHY NOT BE A T-SHIRT EVANGELIST FOR GOD?

So what is T-shirt evangelism? T-shirt Evangelism is purposefully choosing to wear a Christian T-shirt while going about your everyday life and expecting to make an impact on those who see your shirt. You may even choose to wear them to locations your regular day wouldn't normally take you, being lead by the Spirit in your approach. I've seen and heard of some really cool divine appointments that God has orchestrated in the lives of people who wear our shirts. Sometimes you'll get the opportunity to expand upon the message on your tee with someone who asks you about it, and sometimes you won't speak to anyone at all. But the wonderful thing is that as you go about your day, you will have many witnessing opportunities when someone simply reads what your shirt says—without even saying a word. Remember, studies estimate that the average printed T-shirt is read as many as three thousand times before it wears out. That's life-changing and world-changing potential!

When you stand in line at the store, cheer at your child's soccer game, or walk the halls of your school, you are sowing seeds of God's grace, love, and truth. That kid sitting behind you in school is soaking in the truth of the gospel right there in class. Your neighbor who is going through a family crisis can see words of encouragement as you chat across your driveway—these encounters are often more powerful than you will ever know. You and your T-shirt may be the only "Jesus" they will see. The Scripture on your shirt may be the only "Bible" they will read.

Survey

WE'VE ALWAYS KNOWN THAT Christian T-shirts with God's Word on them make an impact because of personal experiences and the many letters and emails we've received from wearers over the years describing how Christian T-shirts have helped them share their faith. But we wanted know more about their effects. Not long ago we conducted a survey among people who regularly wear Christian T-shirts and asked them several questions about their motives and results of wearing them.

We learned some remarkable things from our survey! We learned that 98 percent of those surveyed wear Christian T-shirts in order to share their faith and not just as a fashion statement. Almost half the people surveyed said they've been able to share Christ with an unbeliever because the message on their T-shirt sparked a conversation. And get this! One in fourteen reported that they've helped an unbeliever reach a decision to accept Jesus Christ as their Savior after having a conversation that began because they decided to put on a Christian T-shirt!

Why do fellow believers wear our products? It's not just because they're cool or because they love the designs—it's because overwhelmingly they want to share the gospel. They see the act of putting on that T-shirt as a step in the process of fulfilling that "Great Commission"—telling the world about God and the relationship available with Him through His Son, Jesus. They are T-shirt Evangelists! As you read some of their stories, it's our hope that you will want to be a T-shirt Evangelist too!

THERE IS NOTHING SO ENCOURAGING AS HEARING FROM A "Kerusso Wearer." Sometimes we get a letter or an e-mail; sometimes someone takes the time to visit our Facebook page and post a note telling us of his or her experiences while wearing our apparel. Sometimes we get to hear it straight from their mouths. I was doing an interview on a radio call-in show when Jerry called the station to share his experiences as a T-shirt evangelist;

"I wanted to take the opportunity to encourage all the listeners to take their witness to the next level—to encourage them not to be intimidated or timid about it. Look around you. Guys are wearing T-shirts showing beer ads and things you really don't want to see, and we need men coming from a godly perspective to counter this culture. I started wearing Christian tees a few years ago, and at first I was worried about what people would think about me when I was wearing them. The good news is that the responses that you get are not at all fearful. People will come up to you and even ask what the shirt message means. Sometimes they tell me that they like my shirt. These conversations that I have had in the last 2–3 years have

given me more opportunities to share the gospel than I can even count. One of the things I do before I put on a Christian T-shirt is to talk with God and say, 'God, who do you want me to visit today with this message?' My heart is saying, 'Okay, Lord, I'm ready!' If someone you know has even mentioned the idea of wearing a Christian T-shirt—go get it for them. It could be the step forward they need to get started in sharing the gospel.

Be encouraged, guys. Don't be afraid. Go do it!"

JERRY—T-SHIRT EVANGELIST

ON
AIR

JESUS IS OUR GREATEST

HOPE

WE WAIT FOR THE BLESSED HOPE, THE GLORIOUS APPEARING OF OUR GREAT GOD AND SAVIOR, JESUS CHRIST.
TITUS 2:2

IN GOD

PROVERBS 3:5

I TRUST

TRUST IN THE LORD with all your heart and lean not on your own understanding

Jesus

SWEET SAVIOR

KING OF KINGS

NOT EVERYONE SHARES THEIR FAITH IN THE SAME WAY, AND NOT everyone does T-shirt evangelism the same way either. Jerry prays up and heads out, prepared to have a conversation—the message on his T-shirt the conduit for his boldness. He is looking for specific opportunities. Some people, like Harry Pinchon, just want to wear the message and see what happens, ready to talk about Jesus and take the Good News wherever he goes.

"I'm 68 years old and have been 'born again' about forty years. I have been sending out printed tracts for years, but I like sharing the gospel by wearing tees about Jesus too. I take the city bus to do my errands. We have a transfer center downtown, and I get to talk to a lot of people about my shirts. I like "In God I Trust" because it has a very bold appearance and a rich color that makes it stand out. "Sweet Savior" is colorful and you can read it from a distance. I also like "Jesus Is our Hope." It's very colorful and gets the message across in a unique way."

HENRY PINCHON—T-SHIRT EVANGELIST

A LITTLE LIGHT AT THE BEAUTY SHOP

"I have a wonderful testimony from wearing Kerusso shirts! I attend a cosmetology school. Everyone knows that beauty shops are known for their gossip. On Saturdays we get to wear a black T-shirt of some sort. This past Saturday I wore my Kerusso shirt that says 'A Blood Donor Saved My Life' on the front and a cross with Matthew 26:28 written inside it on the back. I was just minding my own business and doing my work when a fellow student said, 'Candice, did a blood donor really save your life?' I said 'Yes!!' She was like, 'Well, when, and who was it?!' I said, 'A little while back, and His name is Jesus.' She didn't know what to say just looked at me funny; then she began to read the back of my shirt and it hit her, Jesus Christ! So I got to minister to her and the clients that were there about Jesus and how He died for all of us! It was a wonderful time and a great conversation-opener about Jesus! So thank you all for the shirts you make. I enjoy being a 'walking ministry' for Jesus!"

CANDICE—T-SHIRT EVANGELIST VIA FACEBOOK

SOME STORIES JUST BLOW ME AWAY. THEY REMIND ME THAT we serve a God who has impeccable timing. How incredible is it that someone is in just the right spot at just the right time. How amazing is it that we produce that particular shirt at just the right time. How humbling to be part of God's plan!

"God works in amazing ways! Little did I know that the bright red 3:16 Numbers of Hope T-shirt I decided to wear one day was going to make such a difference to a person's life. A woman approached me while we were at McDonald's and asked me without hesitation, 'What does 3:16 mean?' I was somewhat surprised, completely caught unawares, and before I could answer, she explained that for the past two weeks prior to that moment, she had had the same dream every night…with the numbers 3:16 distinct in all of them! So I shared the verse and turned around for her to read it as it was written on the back of the shirt. I told her that it was probably the most famous Scripture and where she could find it in the Bible. This whole encounter took only 5 minutes, but that's all that was needed for the Lord

to do His work! It left me in goose bumps and still does every time I share this small but awesome testimony. Praise God! He totally orchestrated the whole thing...and a humble T-shirt was instrumental in bringing a seeking heart to Him! "

ESTHER RONDAY—T-SHIRT EVANGELIST,
NEW SOUTH WALES, AUSTRALIA

ARE YOU A CHRISTIAN?

"I was wearing a Kerusso T-shirt while out shopping the other day. A lady was looking very lost and despondent, so I stopped and offered her some help. I ended up talking with her for about five minutes—you know, just chatting. She read my shirt and asked if I was a Christian. That let me open the conversation about Jesus. That dear lady ended up giving her life to Christ!"

SOMEONE **IS** SEARCHING FOR YOU
For the Son of Man has come to seek and to save that which was lost.
Luke 19:10

"You guys have taken sharing the word about Jesus to a whole new level. Your products make it easy to share the Word in my everyday life. I own your "How Jesus Saved the World" T-shirt, and it reminds me every day who I should keep first in my life and who I should keep praising in everything that I do. Thank you for helping me to spread the word of our Savior."

ANOTHER T-SHIRT EVANGELIST

HOW JESUS SAVED THE WORLD

Christ died for our sins according to the Scriptures. He was buried, and He was raised on the third day.

"DO YOU REALLY BELIEVE THAT STUFF?"

"Your company and products are a real answer to my prayers! I've had people read my shirts and say, 'Do you really believe that stuff?' and then I get to tell them about the hope we have as Christians. Wearing your shirts allows me many more opportunities to share the good news of Jesus Christ than I would have had otherwise. That's why I love to wear them! It is going to be a very rare occasion that I'm ever caught wearing anything other than a Kerusso Christian T-shirt."

JEFF HARRIS, WORSHIP LEADER AND LEAD GUITARIST FOR SADDLEBACK CHURCH'S OVERDRIVE VENUE.

"Thank you, Kerusso, for your musically themed Christian T-shirts! My son Trey and I play and attend various music events. We wear them and give some away as part of our ministry. It's amazing to see conversations develop with the recipients regarding God and their faith. Jesus said He would make us fishers of men. We view sharing the shirts as throwing the hook in the water; God's will through the conviction of the Holy Spirit takes it from there! We simply study to show ourselves approved unto God to be prepared to share the hope that is within us. Thank you for your obedience to the vision God gave you by providing T-shirts that honor Him and help build the kingdom of God by ministering to others.

May God continue to bless your business abundantly!"

DON SEARCY—CARROLLTON, TX

"My mom isn't a big T-shirt fan—I guess she just doesn't like the way they look on her, but I gave her one of your tees anyway and she felt obligated to wear it.

She wore it to her exercise class one day and it sparked up a conversation with one of the other ladies there. One thing lead to another and Mom invited her to church. The lady she met and her husband ended up coming to church and home fellowship with my mom because she decided to wear the shirt I gave her. I thought that was pretty cool and had to share it with you! God is really working on that couple."

PAUL BASS—T-SHIRT EVANGELIST

"JESUS JUNK"?

IN THE LATE '90'S, WE DECIDED TO EXPAND OUR PRODUCT OFFERING
to include non-apparel items. We began to develop jewelry, gifts, and accessories using the same impactful messages that adorned our shirts and caps. Today we offer a wide range of products that unashamedly share a message of truth and hope with a world that is hurting and broken. Our tote bags, drumsticks, wallets, bracelets, necklaces, guitar picks, guitar straps, and more—are all designed to be a witness to the world and an encouragement to the user. Some have carelessly labeled this sort of thing as "Jesus junk," but we certainly don't see it that way. The intent and often-produced result is a conversation about Jesus.

What follows is a great example of how God uses all kinds of things to reach those in need.

On Wednesday, March 30, 2005, Preston Repass of Richmond, Va., began his day like he has many others—connecting Christian bookstores with the products they need—when he was interrupted by the ultimate sales call. This was a divine appointment where the words he spoke and product he delivered brought life to an unknown bystander in need.

The 47-year-old sales rep was traveling scenic Interstate 64 between Beckley and Covington, Va., en route to customers. As he approached a bridge, he noticed a young man running down the side of the road toward his car. As his car edged closer, the man jumped over the bridge's railing and stood facing the river below.

Repass quickly pulled his car to the side of the road and jumped the railing too.

The troubled man in his mid- to late-20s blurted out, " 'Leave me alone; I have nothing to live for,' " Repass recalled. "As soon as he said that, 'Live for Him' hit me," Repass said, referring to Kerusso's "Live for Him" red wristband project with those words etched in rubber. "I said, 'Hang on, I've got something I want to show you in my car.' "

Repass stepped back over the railing, popped his trunk, pulled out a bracelet, and cautiously edged closer to the man until finally he was able to hand it to him. " 'Look at what this says,' " he remembered. " 'It says to live for Him. Everybody has something to live for.' "

Within minutes of the brief encounter, another car stopped. The man's friends—traveling the same stretch of road on their way home from work—saw his car at the side of the road and were able to coax him off the bridge.

As the friends drove the man away, Repass handed him his business card.

" 'When you get home and start thinking about this day I want you to give me a call so I can explain what the bracelet means,' " Repass said, adding that the man had already slipped the bracelet on.

The next weekend, while Repass was on a boat out of cell phone range, the man did call and leave a message. He didn't leave his name or number, but said that he was okay and would call again. Repass is hoping he does.

Looking back on the event, Repass is thankful for the part God allowed him to play in saving this man's life. "I think the Lord had me there just long enough to detain him until his friends came by," he said. "He looked like he was really on his way." Repass went on to say, "On the day that this

happened I was actually feeling a
bit down myself, so to think that
God would use me to reach someone
who was a lot more down than myself was
a huge encouragement."

The son of a preacher has often had the opportunity to share his faith, but never when combined with his profession. "I've never had the opportunity to use a product that I'm selling to witness to anyone on a one-on-one basis," he said.

Repass looks at his job as his ministry and is always looking for ways to minister through his job. He tells people, "We're going to heaven and we need to take someone with us."

The Kerusso wristband that he gave away that day was a sample, the only one he had with him after the popular wristbands continuously sold out at the stores he served.

"I'm proud to have that product in my bag," Repass said. "It's amazing, the impact that a $1.99 bracelet can have on a single life."

The "Live for Him" red wristband continues to minister and touch lives here in the states and abroad. To date, Kerusso has sold over 1.3 million wristbands, raising over $375,000 for Compassion International.

CHANGE YOUR SHIRT—CHANGE YOUR SCHOOL...

Tyler's #1 goal was to win more of his friends to Christ.

"I wanted to thank you for giving my son, Tyler, a resource to show his faith! The first day of 8th grade last year, Tyler was given a project in Language Arts. He had to write down two goals they had for that year and how they were going to accomplish them. Tyler's #1 goal was to win more of his friends to Christ. How was he going to accomplish this? —He was going to wear a Christian T-shirt to school every day. He has worn a Christian T-shirt to school every day since the 8th grade. He just started high school, and I asked him if he was going to continue wearing his T-shirts to school. His response was, 'Yeah, Mom, don't you think high schoolers need God in their lives even more than middle schoolers do?' Well, that's my boy! Always thinking of others. Well, Tyler is continually working on his friends and trying to be a role model to his peers. He gets questioned about his shirts a lot and it gives him an opportunity to share his faith. I could go on and on about his servant's heart. But my main purpose of writing this letter was to thank you for providing a way for Tyler to share his faith with other students! You are such a blessing! Thanks for listening, and keep up the good work!"

TAMMY CROWDER ABOUT HER SON,
TYLER—T-SHIRT EVANGELIST

"I only wear Christian shirts to school..."

"I love all your shirts! I think they are ingenious and the perfect way to spread the Word. I only wear Christian shirts to school, and every day my classmates look forward to seeing my shirts. Yet some kids complain and always ask me when I will ever wear just a plain shirt. But that doesn't stop me and I wear them anyway. I think they're starting to like my shirts too!"

MATT RIVERA—T-SHIRT EVANGELIST

"Why are you wearing such a lie?"

"I live in Australia and my friend got me a T-shirt from Kerusso, and I just want more of them... They are really awesome. I love seeing the look on people's faces when they see a young teenager walking down the street with a T-shirt that tells people that Jesus died for us and he loves us. I have even had a few encounters with people who ask, "Why are you wearing such a lie?" and they have gone away considering what I say to them. It's amazing how much a few words on a T-shirt can change a person's perspective on life forever.... :)

LYNDAL WILSON—T-SHIRT EVANGELIST

"You CAN change the world!"

"Kerusso T-shirts have been a great way for me to witness at school. People comment on them almost every day. I found out that a student in my school was saved recently, partly because of seeing my shirts on a daily basis! I truly believe that by changing your shirt, you CAN change the world!"

HIGH SCHOOL T-SHIRT EVANGELIST

"I'm a 35-year-old resident of Carlyle, IL, and I love to wear your T-shirts! It's great to see people take that second glance! By wearing your shirts I've really multiplied the amount of people that I expose to Jesus on a daily basis. Even if it's only a glimpse at a T-shirt, people get exposed, and that's what it's all about anyway, right? I look forward to adding more shirts to my collection. Thank you all for not being afraid to stand up for what we believe in. It helps empower me to do the same. God bless you all."

CHRISTIAN HOLLENKAMP—T-SHIRT EVANGELIST

LOVE BUILT A BRIDGE

"I wanted you to see what kind of an impact we are having with your products.

A teenage girl and her mother were walking past my store in the mall. The young lady wanted to stop and look at the Kerusso shirts I have on display. Her mother did not want to stop and look. I could gather by the comments I overheard that it was because of their Christian content.

I asked the mom to read the back of the "Love Built a Bridge" shirt in an attempt to slow her down and allow her daughter some time to look. As she read it, her face clouded and she started to cry. I asked her if I could pray with her. She said yes and accepted Jesus Christ as she stood here in front of my store!

When she regained her composure a bit, she related to me that in the past year, her husband had walked out on the family. Her tears began to flow again as she described finding her 17-yr-old daughter dead in her room just four months ago.

She had approached the brink of suicide often in the past months and felt that her 13-year-old daughter was the only reason she had to continue living.

Mother and daughter went on their way through the mall.

The exuberance that young girl showed at her mom's transformation was the most precious gift I'll receive this Christmas. Before they left the mall that day, they came back and brought me a cookie from the food court and many, many thanks for being there with that shirt and my prayer.

Keep up the good work, all! "

BILL SULLIVAN—STORE OWNER

HEAVY DRINKER?

I LOVE HEARING THESE STORIES from friends and fans who wear our shirts! To actually get to hear about the fruit of your kingdom labor is an honor and a treat.

I wear our shirts a lot but get the most reactions to them when I travel. I love seeing people's eyes as they read my shirts! Most of the verbal responses I get are simple *"I like your shirt!"* comments, usually from fellow believers voicing their support. But I've also had my share of other interactions, like the time I was in Las Vegas for a trade show with my wife.

We were staying at one of the hotel and casinos on the strip and I was walking through the lobby, heading to the gym for a workout. I was wearing one of our shirts, which, like many, is intended to get a good "double take" from whoever might read it. The shirt I put on that day wasn't chosen by accident. The front of the shirt said **HEAVY DRINKER**, with the Scripture reference of John 7:37 boldly underneath it. The intent of the front of the shirt is to get that double take and really turn a head yet hint that this is no ordinary "drinker's shirt." The back of the shirt has the last half of John 7:37 (KJV) written out for the world to see:

"IF ANY MAN THIRST, LET HIM COME UNTO ME, AND DRINK."

So on my way to the gym, walking through the lobby of the casino, a guy who had clearly been doing drinking of another kind read the front of my shirt and said, "Right on, man! That's what I'm talkin' about." I told him he wasn't getting the point, and I turned around to let him read the back of my shirt. With a much less boisterous reply he said, "Yah, I guess that's cool too."

SEED SOWN!

This guy wasn't expecting a sermon that day—not even a mini sermon delivered by a T-shirt and the guy wearing it! But that's exactly what he got.

Did his life change? Maybe, maybe not. But I know this—he had to deal with what he read on my shirt, and here's what God has to say about that:

HEAVY DRINKER

John 7:37

"IF ANY MAN THIRST, LET HIM COME UNTO ME, AND DRINK."

-JESUS

> **"SO SHALL MY WORD BE THAT GOES FORTH FROM MY MOUTH; IT SHALL NOT RETURN TO ME VOID, BUT IT SHALL ACCOMPLISH WHAT I PLEASE, AND IT SHALL PROSPER IN THE THING FOR WHICH I SENT IT."**
>
> **ISAIAH 55:11 (NKJV)**

If we wait inside our churches to reach the lost, we will never reach them. They aren't inside the church (for the most part); **they're in the lobby of the casino,** the mall, the gym, the grocery store, the DMV line, the airport, the school, and pretty much everywhere else your day might take you.

As the body of Christ we should carry the light of God with us everywhere we go and we can and should be that light with or without a Christian T-shirt on. But I know that wearing a good message from God into the world is an effective way to reach even more people and sow more seeds than if you don't.

The simple decision of which shirt or hat I'm going to wear when I go to the gym today might be a really big deal to the people who will read it. It could be the difference between happiness or sorrow, a fight with their spouse tonight, not, a hug for their child or a cruel word—or worse. It might make the difference for someone to praise and thank God rather than grumble and complain.

For some, it will mean the difference between eternal joy in the presence of God and His Son Jesus, or eternal suffering and sorrow without Him.

Friends, God doesn't charge us with the results of preaching His Word—He just said to do it!

1 Corinthians 3:6 KJV says, **"I have planted, Apollos watered; but God gave the increase."** You see, God takes care of the results; He just wants us to preach —to **"kerusso"** the good news.

Consider Romans 10:13–15: **"For 'Everyone who calls on the name of the Lord will be saved.' But how can they call on him to save them unless they believe in him? And how can they believe in him if they have never heard about him? And how can they hear about him unless someone tells them? And how will anyone go and tell them unless they are sent?"** (NLT).

If you're a child of God, you've been sent! Jesus said in Mark 16:15 to GO into all the world and tell the good news to everyone! **So let's do it!**

Let's change our shirts and change the world!

This T-shirt was produced from 2009 to 2011.

FIREPROOF

"FIREPROOF"
BY KIRK CAMERON

In the hit movie *Fireproof* I took on the role
Fire Chief Caleb Holt. The opening scene
shows Caleb and the firemen fighting a fully
developed house fire. Firemen are trained to
work in pairs when they enter a building like
this. But in that scene, one of the men leaves
his partner alone in the building, putting him
at greater risk. When they all safely return to
the firehouse, my character Caleb reprimands
him for not following protocol and tells him,
"You never leave your partner."
Writers Alex and Stephen Kendrick used this
analogy to remind us that marriage is supposed
to be like that.

God gave us the example not long after He created Adam and Eve in the garden, way back in Genesis 2:24, when He said, "Therefore shall a man leave his father and his mother, and shall cleave unto his wife: and they shall be one flesh." (KJV) That word "cleave" in the Hebrew literally means to be joined together, never to come apart.

KIRK CAMERON is an actor who starred on the sitcom *Growing Pains* from 1985–1992 and in several hit films including *Fireproof*. He is an associate with evangelist Ray Comfort for The Way of the Master and also founded Camp Firefly with his wife, actress Chelsea Noble. Learn more about what Kirk is doing at www.kirkcameron.com.

That theme—never leave your partner—is needed now more than ever. With the world "burning down" morally, there's a "disposable-marriage" mind-set that has become commonplace in our culture. That's not God's best for our lives! God wants us to be totally loyal to our spouses for the duration - for our own good.

In Ephesians 5:25, the great apostle Paul, by inspiration of the Holy Spirit says, "Husbands, love your wives, just as Christ loved the church and gave himself up for her." (NIV) He points to the example Jesus gave us—the ultimate sacrifice He made for His bride, the church, of laying down His very life!

The character from the movie had a number of marriage problems, but through prayer and with God's help, he made the choice to have a God-centered marriage that put God and wife first, laying down his own selfish desires. This is a legacy that I very much want to leave my family! Ultimate loyalty comes from Jesus Christ.

I've made that choice and pray and work on it every day, and you can too!

Fireproof title treatment and images used by arrangement with Sherwood Pictures/Provident Film

ON THE 6TH DAY,
GOD CREATED
DINOSAURS!

Kerusso

GENESIS 1:24

This T-shirt was introduced in 2007

DINOSAURS...
ON THE
SIXTH DAY?

BY JOHN MORRIS

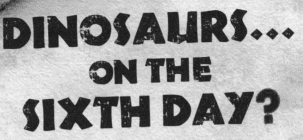

From an early age we were taught, "Millions of years ago dinosaurs ruled the earth." Did we ever stop to wonder:

How do "they" know?

Was anyone around to make such an observation, or is this simply an opinion of scientists about the unobserved past? Scientific statements should be founded on observation, not just opinions, even opinions of "experts."

Thankfully we do have a record of the past written by a trustworthy observer, the Bible. It surprises many to learn that Scripture often mentions dinosaur-like beasts. In Genesis 1 we read that all things were created during Creation week, not very long ago– a teaching reinforced in the Ten Commandments (Exodus 20:11). This includes dinosaurs! They weren't called dinosaurs, for that term wasn't "invented" until the mid-1800s. Instead, Scripture refers to them as "dragons" or "beasts of the earth," etc. Precise descriptions of amazing creatures named "Behemoth" and "Leviathan" can be read in Job 40: 15-24 and 41:1-34. Furthermore the history of almost every culture includes dragon - like beasts, reptilian creatures with tfearsome teeth, long necks, and armored sides, etc.

Without a doubt, dinosaur and man lived at the same time.

We should trust the clear statements of an eyewitness, One who can make good observations and is completely trustworthy. In Scripture He tells us of the time of Creation, when all things were "good" and lived in harmony, including Adam (who was the steward of Creation) and the animals. It also tells (Genesis 3) of the time when Adam rebelled or sinned against God, and how God issued the penalty for sin. "The wages of sin is death," (Romans 6:23 KJV) which applied to all Adam's realm, including Adam's descendants. It also tells us how our sin-penalty was paid by God's only Son, Jesus Christ.

"Christ died for our sins" (I Corinthians 15:3).

As we confess our sins, believing that His work on the cross fully pays for our sins, we can be forgiven and receive eternal life.

Let us understand the truth about dinosaurs, their origin, history, and message. They have much to teach us of our own condition and how we can live forever with the Creator of all.

JOHN MORRIS, president of the Institute for Creation Research—www.icr.org—has a PhD in geology from the University of Oklahoma and is an internationally known author and speaker. His search for Noah's ark on Turkey's Mt. Ararat has yielded fascinating research. He and his wife live in Dallas.

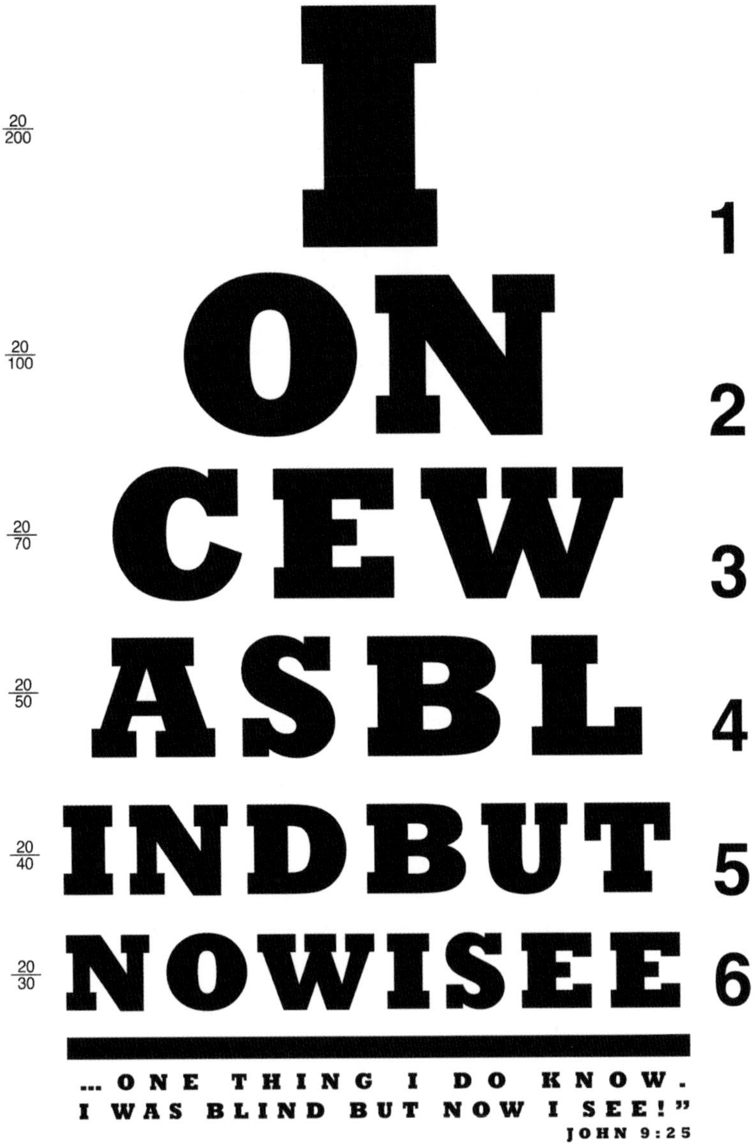
20/200 I 1
20/100 ON 2
20/70 CEW 3
20/50 ASBL 4
20/40 INDBUT 5
20/30 NOWISEE 6
...ONE THING I DO KNOW.
I WAS BLIND BUT NOW I SEE!"
JOHN 9:25

This T-shirt was introduced in 2011.

THE FIRST FACE I'LL SEE IN HEAVEN

BY JENNIFER ROTHSCHILD

I DON'T KNOW WHAT IT'S LIKE ANYMORE TO LOOK INTO PEOPLE'S FACES.

It's been many years since I saw a face clearly due to the blinding effects of my eye disease. As a child I looked into my mother's face, and at her soft olive skin, and I know I looked into the sweetness of my dad's dancing blue eyes and watched his forehead wrinkle when he was in deep thought. I looked into the freckled faces of my sometimes annoying little brothers; I looked into the wise eyes of my beloved grandparents.

Those were the loved ones' faces I saw before blindness. My husband and two sons' faces, I've never seen. What fascinates me is that even though I know I saw all those precious faces, in my memory they are now draped in shadows, blurred and indistinguishable. They are as absent as the faces of my husband and sons. It's heartbreaking, for the memory of faces I love to fade in my mind's eye.

Physical blindness is difficult, that's for sure. But far more devastating is living with spiritual blindness. To allow your circumstances to blind you to the goodness of God is far more debilitating than physical darkness. To silence the voice of God who longs to tell you of His love and forgiveness is far worse than physical deafness. To be paralyzed by fear is far more confining than physical immobility.

Spiritual sight allows us to really see what is beautiful and good—life that cannot be shrouded by darkness, silenced by deafness, or stilled by paralysis.

I once had physical sight, but now I am blind. I once was spiritually blind but through faith in Christ, now I see! (John 9:25).

My spiritual gaze is fixed on the truth that unless God chooses to heal my blindness, the very first face I'll see with clarity will be the face of Jesus.

My friend, when we see His face, every earthly heartache and joy will fade. So ask God to open your spiritual eyes so you can really see.

I ONCE HAD PHYSICAL SIGHT, BUT NOW I AM BLIND. I ONCE WAS SPIRITUALLY BLIND BUT THROUGH FAITH IN CHRIST, NOW I SEE!

Jennifer Rothschild's life drastically changed at the age of fifteen when she lost her sight. Now, more than 30 years later, she boldly and compassionately teaches women how to walk by faith and not by sight. She travels the country offering fresh, sensible biblical advice to audiences who, like her, are determined to pursue healthy and productive lives. Jennifer has shared her inspiring message to arena-sized audiences of the popular Women of Faith conferences and media outlets, including *Dr. Phil, Good Morning America, Life Today,* and *The Billy Graham Television Special.* She's the author of seven books, including the best-selling *Lessons I Learned in the Dark, Self Talk, Soul Talk, Walking by Faith, Me, Myself and Lies* and *Missing Pieces; Real Hope when Life doesn't make Sense.*

Jennifer and her Dr. Phil live in Springfield, Missouri with their two sons, Clayton and Connor.

FOR THE
WEAPONS OF OUR WARFARE
ARE NOT CARNAL, BUT MIGHTY THROUGH GOD TO THE PULLING DOWN OF STRONG HOLDS
2 CORINTHIANS 10:4

CALLED TO DUTY

This T-shirt was
introduced in 2010

GOD'S
WARRIORS

By Lt. General William G. Boykin

The concept of a warrior society is ancient, with many historic examples of nations and people groups who trained constantly for war. As the Spartan king, Leonidas stood before the massed forces of the Persian king, Xerxes, at a small mountain pass called Thermopylae in modern Greece, he knew that his three-hundred men were going to lose the battle, but he refused to surrender. The year was 480 BC, and Xerxes intended to destroy and enslave the citizens of the city-states of Greece.

  Offered leniency by Xerxes if he would lay down his weapons, Leonidas responded with a simple retort: "Molon Lebe." In English, the words mean "Come and take them." Leonidas and his men fought to their deaths over a three-day period, inflicting heavy losses on the Persians and providing the Greeks an opportunity to evacuate their cities and to prepare for a battle a few months later that defeated the combined military forces of the Persians.

Exodus 15:3 says that, "The LORD is a warrior; the LORD is his name." Furthermore, Revelation 19 describes Jesus as a warrior leading a mighty army of His followers as He destroys His enemies. It is important for Christians to understand that we are, in fact, God's army. The Bible tells us that we are always in a spiritual battle—a battle of good against evil. Just as King Leonidas stood against the evil of the Persian Empire, Christians stand against the evil of our enemy, Satan, who the Bible describes as a "roaring lion" who "prowls around… looking for someone to devour" (1 Peter 5:8).

Second Corinthians 10:4 gives us perfect marching orders; it tells us that "the weapons of our warfare" are infinitely more effective than even the best efforts of our technical brains, because they are "mighty through God to the pulling down of strong holds" (KJV).

It is important in our spiritual walk with Christ that we recognize the imperative of being spiritual warriors in His kingdom.

FOR THE WEAPONS OF OUR WARFARE ARE NOT CARNAL, BUT MIGHTY THROUGH GOD TO THE PULLING DOWN OF STRONG HOLDS

2 CORINTHIANS 10:4

JERRY BOYKIN retired from the U.S. Army in 2007, after 36 years of service. In that time, he rose to become Deputy Undersecretary of Defense for Intelligence and U.S. Special Army Operations Command. He was also a member of Delta Force for 15 years. Today, General Boykin is an author and teaches at Hampden-Sydney College, Virginia.

www.KingdomWarriors.net

I ONCE WAS BLIND...

BUT NOW I SEE

DANGER AHEAD

John 9:25

This T-shirt was introduced
in 2012

HOW TO MAKE AN ATHEIST BACKSLIDE

By Ray Comfort

We should never underestimate the power of a few words. "Let there be light," had pretty big repercussions. Words of warning can save lives, and this is true even if they are written on a T-shirt.

Well-placed messages can open a person's eyes to truth. Scripture tells us a remarkable story in the book of John. Jesus had healed a man blind all his life. When questioned by the authorities, the man replied, "One thing I know, that, whereas I was blind, now I see" (KJV).

In his encounter with Jesus, he "got the message," as it were!

A few well-chosen words can also change minds about life and death issues. For example, I once saw a business sign that said, "We would rather do business with one thousand Al Qaeda terrorists than with one American soldier." When I saw that sign, I was furious. I began thinking that these people—whoever they were—didn't deserve to live in this country. Then I saw something that made me do a complete 180. It said, *"We are a funeral home."* When I saw that, I immediately smiled and said, "I *love* these people. God bless them." It was *knowledge* given to me by those few words that gave me another perspective and completely changed my mind, in seconds.

That's what happens when people watch 180movie.com. Eight people who are adamantly pro-abortion become pro-life in seconds because of words that gave knowledge, which gave them another perspective. That gave them their ability to change their minds about the life-and-death issue of abortion.

The same thing can happen with an atheist. Those who embrace atheism think they are intelligent until they hear these few words: "So you believe that nothing created everything—a scientific impossibility?" Say those words to an atheist and watch his facial expression change, as he sees how thoughtless the nature of atheism.

The same principle applies with the gospel, if it's presented biblically. Ask someone if they think that they are a good person, and you will find that they are like the young man who came running to Jesus in Mark 10:17. They have no idea what the word "good" means. So do what Jesus did and ask if he has kept the Ten Commandments. The moral Law gives sinners "knowledge," and that gives them another perspective. Someone may think he is a good person until the Law brings him "the knowledge of sin" (see Romans 3:19, 20, 7:7, 7:13). A few minutes earlier, he thought that he was good and on his way to heaven, but the Law shows him that he's not and that he's on his way to hell. That makes him ask, "What must I do to be saved?" preparing his heart for the good news of the cross. Use words. They *are* necessary. And use them whether they are spoken or written in a book, or on a billboard, or T-shirt.

Born in New Zealand, **RAY COMFORT** is the founder of Living Waters Publications and The Way of the Master Evangelistic ministry. He is well-known as a conference speaker and has written several books. Along with Kirk Cameron, he cohosts The Way of the Master Television Show. He lives in Southern California.

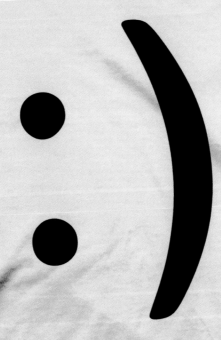

Smile, God Loves You!
John 3:16

This T-shirt was introduced in 2011.

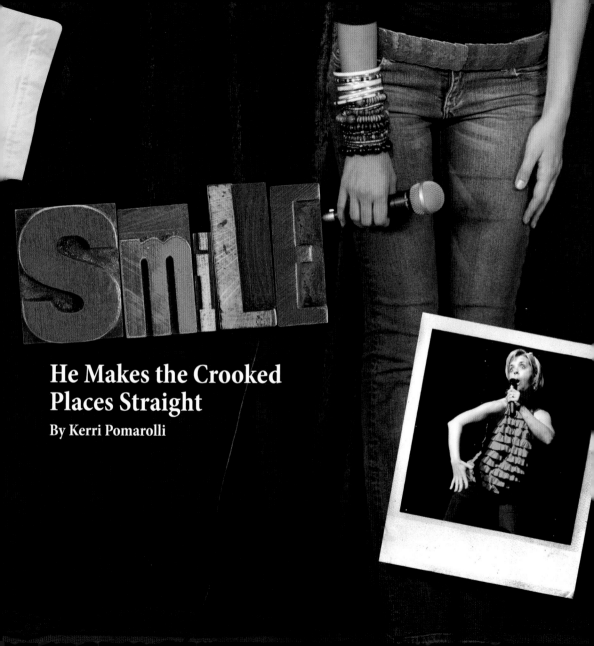

SMILE

He Makes the Crooked
Places Straight

By Kerri Pomarolli

My parents had me telling jokes with punch lines before I was two. I tell them that if they had taught me math, I'd be sending them on cruises right now!

I knew from a very young age that I wanted to be famous. So my mom started me in dance classes by the time I could walk. I was on a fast track to become a professional dancer until I was diagnosed with severe scoliosis, which led to major spinal fusion surgery at age 11.

With my dance career over I poured my life into acting. I landed roles right away in our local theater troupe and went on to tour in Europe and train in London through my college years. As a young woman, I was getting worldly success and my mom had things to brag about at bridge…but I wasn't happy. I silently prayed one night while sitting in a show: "God, I just want to perform. However YOU see fit. I just want to come back to You."

The very next day, things changed. God led me to stand-up comedy! Not only did He want me to talk about HIM, but to do it in Hollywood—where He wasn't getting much stage time.

I ended up with a new career focus: making people laugh. Never in my wildest dreams would I have imagined I'd be a stand-up comedian!

I've gotten to pray for people all over the world, sometimes in late-night clubs or bars where God really needs to do some healing—letting people know how Jesus really did die for their sins and it isn't just a story.

Life is funny. I have to smile about it all now, and as a Christian I smile most when I think of what Christ did for us and how God loves us (John 3:16). He even let me put all my angst as a young woman to good use—plenty of stand-up material!

So don't go looking to be someone else. Just ask God to show you all the amazing things about you. **He also promises to "make the crooked places in our lives straight"! We just have to be willing to be flexible!**

KERRI POMAROLLI graduated from the University of Michigan and studied theater in London before embarking on a spectacular comedy/acting career. Her credits include The *Tonight Show*, CBN, *Comedy Central*, and many others. She is also an author and a much-sought-after speaker. But her best gig is at home with her comedian husband, Ron McGehee, and their two daughters, Lucy and Ruby Joy. www.kerripom.com.

ARMY OF THE ONE

"THE LORD OUR GOD IS ONE!"

MARK 12:29

This T-shirt was produced from 2001 to 2009

AN ARMY OF ONE?

BY JOSEPH S. BONSALL

All my life, I've loved veterans, patriotism, and this wonderful country that God allows us to live in.

When I saw the Kerusso shirt "Army of THE One," it took my breath away,

because it encapsulates everything our brave men and women have defended for 200-plus years!

My own dad was a war veteran and a hero in my eyes. He was wounded during the D-Day landings, and he not only carried the wounds with him, he became one of those whose sacrifice sent him on a detour of life. My sweet mother tended to him for many years and they managed just fine. The reason? They actually believed that if you are in the army of "The One," you *can* meet any challenge! My sweet mama and daddy lived out their lives in Philly and never missed an opportunity to tell folks that Jesus Christ is the only Commander you need in the journey you've been set on.

I've thought of that many times over the years as the Oak Ridge Boys have toured the world. I'll let you in on a little secret: our favorite events and crowds always have veterans in them. And more often than not, when we sing about faith, family, and country, these vets shout out how they feel about the God who's been so good to us!

I didn't always want to be a soldier in God's army. Like so many, I sowed wild oats and all that, but in those dark hours we all have from time to time, my General always heard my cries and pitiful pleas for help. As I've gotten older and learned to appreciate more the quieter things of life, I've realized that my real purpose here is to sing and tell these heartfelt stories of sacrifice from our veterans… so that someone will come to Jesus. And as one who fancies himself a writer and storyteller, the message of Mark 12:29 dovetails perfectly with how I now view the world and my place in it. At the end of my road, it won't matter how many people have heard me and my dear, wonderful buddies sing over the years, or how many Gold records we've attained and all that.

The only thing that will matter is that this vulnerable "Oak" has been sheltered by the true, living God. His shade and provision have sustained me even in those years when I wasn't thinking too much about Him. That is why I'm proud to serve in His army!

JOE BONSALL is a longtime member of The Oak Ridge Boys and the author of several books, including *G.I. Joe & Lillie: Remembering a Life of Love and Loyalty* and *From My Perspective*. Joe lives in Hendersonville, Tennessee, with his wife Mary Ann and their eight cats, Sunny, Sally Ann, Ted, Baybé, Blackie, Callie, Crockett, and LT. He and Mary also spend a lot of time at their 400-acre farm on the Tennessee-Kentucky state line.

www.josephsbonsall.com

JESUS
HEALS

BROKEN
HEARTS

HE HEALS THE BROKENHEARTED AND
BINDS UP THEIR WOUNDS. – PSALM 147:3

This T-shirt was
introduced in 2011.

JESUS HEALS BROKEN HEARTS

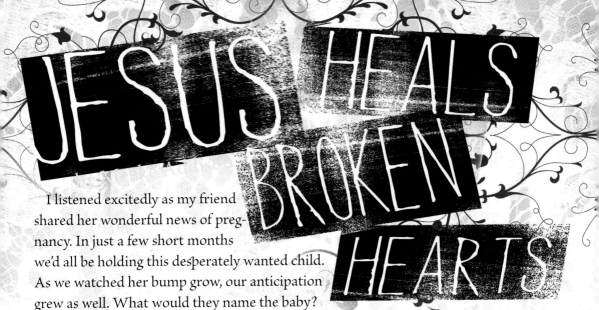

I listened excitedly as my friend shared her wonderful news of pregnancy. In just a few short months we'd all be holding this desperately wanted child. As we watched her bump grow, our anticipation grew as well. What would they name the baby? Was it a boy or girl? Would they find out the gender or wait and be surprised? They were quite surprised. At a routine checkup the doctor couldn't find a heartbeat. A follow-up ultrasound revealed the lifeless body of the baby my friend and her husband had already welcomed into their home. Brokenhearted is insufficient in describing what they felt.

His promise was the forever kind; the 'til-death-do-we-part type. So they set out on a journey together with the wind at their backs and the Son ahead. Sure, there would be setbacks but nothing they couldn't overcome together... together. One day her husband accidentally sent her a text message meant for someone else. No big deal except that it described his affection for another woman. "What happened? Where did our commitment fail? What does this mean?" she wondered. If a heart could be detected inside her chest, it was indeed broken.

When the heart breaks, the first question is usually, "Why"? But immediately following that, the question is "How"? How will I go on? How can I trust Him? How can I make sure this never happens again? While the answers to our whys often don't come quickly or at all, the answers to our hows are more easily accessible. Jesus heals the brokenhearted. In fact I'm humbled that a specific part of His mission, the reason He was sent, was to heal the brokenhearted. Jesus said of Himself in Luke 4:18, "The Spirit of the Lord is upon Me, because He has anointed Me to preach the gospel to the poor; He has sent Me to heal the brokenhearted" (NKJV).

You and your fragile heart matter to God. You matter so much that He commissioned His Son to specialize in broken hearts. Don't hide your disappointments. Don't pretend the hurts didn't, for God is near to those who have a broken heart. **The process isn't easy or quick, but when you press into Him you will discover the miracle that is Jesus healing your broken heart.**

MEEKE ADDISON is a radio and TV personality. She is the host of "Meeke," a TV talk show produced by American Family Association (AFA) and Christian Television Network (CTN). She is a wife and mom of three and resides in Tupelo, Mississippi. Learn more about Meeke and her ministry at www.meeke.org.

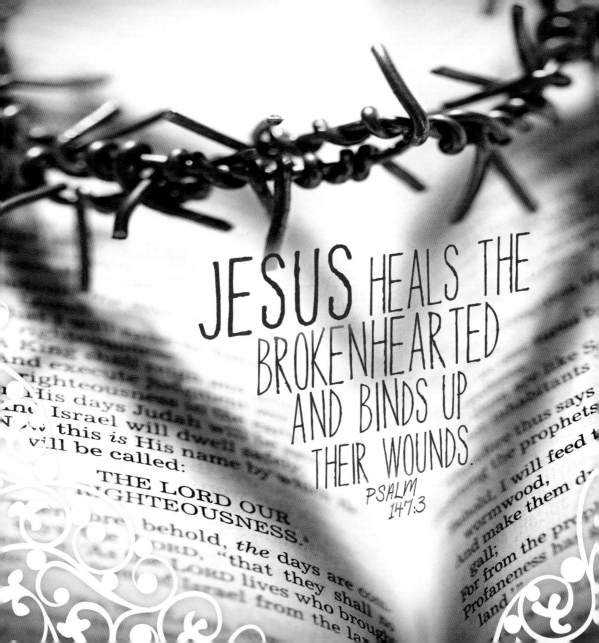

JESUS HEALS THE BROKENHEARTED AND BINDS UP THEIR WOUNDS.

PSALM 147:3

GIVING BACK

God has much to say about giving and helping others. He teaches us through His Word that He's pleased when we share our kindness and material blessings with others. Here are a few examples:

If you help the poor, you are lending to the Lord—and he will repay you!

PROVERBS 19:17 (NLT)

Remember this—a farmer who plants only a few seeds will get a small crop. But the one who plants generously will get a generous crop. You must each decide in your heart how much to give. And don't give reluctantly or in response to pressure. "For God loves a person who gives cheerfully." And God will generously provide all you need. Then you will always have everything you need and plenty left over to share with others. As the Scriptures say, "They share freely and give generously to the poor. Their good deeds will be remembered forever."

2 CORINTHIANS 9:6–11 (NLT)

"Then the King will say to those on his right, 'Come, you who are blessed by my Father; take your inheritance, the kingdom prepared for you since the creation of the world. For I was hungry and you gave me something to eat, I was thirsty and you gave me something to drink, I was a stranger and you invited me in, I needed clothes and you clothed me, I was sick and you looked after me, I was in prison and you came to visit me.' Then the righteous will answer him, 'Lord, when did we see you hungry and feed you, or thirsty and give you something to drink? When did we see you a stranger and invite you in, or needing clothes and clothe you? When did we see you sick or in prison and go to visit you?' The King will reply, 'Truly I tell you, whatever you did for one of the least of these brothers and sisters of mine, you did for me.'"

MATTHEW 25:34–40 (NIV)

When we give of our time and material blessings to those in need, Jesus says we are doing it unto Him. That really makes you want to do more, doesn't it?

God has blessed Kerusso over the years, and we haven't taken His words about sharing those blessings with people in need lightly.

9-11-2001

On September 11, 2001, like everyone else in America, we were glued to our televisions as we watched the day's events with a mix of horror and sadness. Like a lot of people, I watched those scenes and felt compelled to find a way to help. In the days that followed we were swept up in the desire to express our love of our country and countrymen and decided that we could quickly design a line of patriotic tees to encourage and reassure the reader. We could use these tees to raise funds specifically to help in this time of need. Our sales team mobilized and got the shirts out quickly, and by Christmas that year we were able to raise $15,000! We sent funds to the Salvation Army and the American Red Cross disaster relief funds. This event opened my eyes to a huge potential to make a difference in a tangible way on a larger scale.

He Loves

He Listens

He Restores

He Remembers

REMEMBER
SEPTEMBER
9/11/01

THE ULTIMATE

SACRIFICE

"No greater love has anyone than this, that he lay down his life for another."
JOHN 15:3

SCARS & STRIPES

FOREVER

"If the Son sets you free, you are free indeed." JOHN 8:39

WHEN DISASTERS STRIKE

Tornadoes, hurricanes, earthquakes—when disasters like these occur, thousands of people can be left with nothing. The needs are real and they are urgent! Many times, as an apparel company, we've seen the need for emergency clothing and have sprung into action when we could. Our hope is that our tees not only clothe those in need, but that their messages offer the recipients hope and tell them who to turn to in these tragic times. Over the years we've literally shipped tons of T-shirts to help clothe the survivors of the Haiti earthquake, Hurricanes Katrina and Ike, and the killer tornadoes that ravaged the south in 2011.

When Hurricane Ike devastated the Louisiana and Texas coast, we felt compelled to act. The needs were huge within metro areas like Galveston and Houston. Haiti was pounded by storms and floods from Ike. We partnered with Convoy of Hope and Catholic Charities to mobilize a massive shipment of clothing—over 20,000 tees! In

the months that followed, we would hear from people who had been touched by the messages on our tees. In the wake of something massive our efforts can seem inconsequential, but knowing that those messages are out there at a time like that, turning people's thoughts to our loving Creator, was humbling. Fifteen months after Ike hit Haiti, it was hit once again with a devastating earthquake. We worked again with Convoy of Hope to get 4,000 more T-shirts out to the people of Haiti, on some of the first transports going to the island nation.

2011 TORNADOS

In the Spring of 2011, horrible tornadoes struck the Tuscaloosa, Alabama, and Joplin, Missouri areas. The images on our televisions showed picturesque countrysides much like our own ravaged by the paths of these powerful storms. Over 300 people lost their lives, and thousands of homes and businesses were damaged and destroyed.

We quickly mobilized truckloads containing over 15,000 T-shirts for those who were left without even the basics. Our shirts were used in packs containing food and household items, the kinds of things you need to get by on until the insurance company claims are paid. The Joplin storm, in particular, hit very close to home. Joplin is in the Ozarks, just an hour and a half away from Kerusso's headquarters. In addition to sending T-shirts, teams of Kerusso employees volunteered their weekends to help out. Seeing the damage done by that EF-5 storm was unbelievable—a path of destruction over a mile wide ran right through the heart of the city. It looked like a war zone. Over the summer many Kerusso team members would reach out to their neighbors to the north, helping them to dig out and start over. Being there on the ground, helping and praying with those who lost so much, was a life-changing thing. Giving is a privilege and a blessing. Once you do it, you want to give more.

Team Kerusso praying over a shipment of t-shirts headed to Haiti.

LIVE FOR HIM

In 2005, we began to notice all the "cause" wristbands hitting the market, a phenomenon that was started by Lance Armstrong and Nike's Live Strong campaign and donated money to cancer research for every wristband purchased. We like to be on the front end of product trends, so my team jumped on the idea of developing one for our line. As I thought about this, I was impressed that we needed to find an impeccable charity where some of the proceeds from this product could be donated. After much research and prayer, we decided on **Compassion International**. As I learned more about their organization, I became more determined than ever to try to make something big happen with those little wristbands. I felt the Lord put a big number on my heart. I gathered the design and marketing teams in our conference room and told them that I wanted to set a goal of raising $500,000 for Compassion! The team was a little shocked but they all came together. Wristbands, packaging, PR, advertising—everyone pulling together. We asked ourselves what kind of statement would work on a wristband to drive home the project. **Live For Him** was the title and theme we chose. Customers could wear a band as a symbol of their desire to live for Christ. Living for Him also means "giving to the least of these," expressed in Matthew 25:40. It was the perfect fit for the project.

As we worked on this project we saw an interesting side effect. Some of the Kerusso team started sponsoring Compassion children and became even more invested in the success of the project. Sales of the wristbands took off as retailers and consumers joined the cause! By the next summer we were able to present Wess Stafford, Compassion's President, a check for $250,000! To date we have sold well over 1.3 million of those red wristbands, along with thousands of T-shirts, caps, and rings. Because of God's grace and the support of our customers, we've raised over $375,000 for Compassion so far!

Compassion is an amazing organization. It does so much with its resources. Sponsoring a child provides clean water, health care, education, nutrition, and most importantly, biblical teaching and nurturing.

Founded in 1952, Compassion successfully tackles global poverty one child at a time, serving more than one million children in twenty-five of the world's poorest countries. Recognizing that poverty is more than a lack of money, Compassion works holistically through local churches to address the individual physical, economic, educational, and spiritual needs of children—enabling them to thrive, not just survive. Charity Navigator, America's largest charity evaluator, has awarded Compassion its highest rating—four stars—for seven consecutive years.

Handing out LIVE FOR HIM wristbands

In 2006, my son Nik and I traveled with Compassion to Peru. It was a thrilling experience. We were able to see firsthand what good stewards Compassion and their local volunteers are with the resources they are given. We participated in games and programs with hundreds of kids while visiting several Compassion projects in Lima and Cusco. The kids and volunteers treated us like rock stars! They so appreciate their Compassion sponsors. This trip left me more determined than ever to press forward to reach our goal!

Our Sponsor Team at Machu Picchu

We saw firsthand just how
much sponsorship means
for the children of Compassion.

While we were there we decided to personally sponsor two Lima-area children and actually got to meet "our" kids and their families! It was a real blessing. Sponsoring a child is an amazing experience! It's so rewarding to receive their letters and photos telling you about their lives—and being able to share yours with them. Seeing Compassion in action was a gift that I will treasure for the rest of my life. Please consider sponsoring a child. Learn more at **www.compassion.com**.

Class time in Cusco, Peru

Sports Day at the Lima Project

Vic and Nik with their newly sponsored kids and their families

JEREMY'S GREATEST LOVE

When we developed the Live For Him wristband we saw it as having a dual purpose. Of course we wanted it to be used to raise funds for Compassion, but we also wanted it to be something that we could wear all the time to remind us of what we truly live for. Occasionally we hear that it has done so much more. One day we got a call from a woman. Her son's best friend, a 16-year-old boy, had been tragically killed in a skateboarding accident. Jeremy was a believer and NEVER removed his Live For Him wristband. While they were working on him in the ER, his mom pleaded for the doctors to leave it on; it meant everything to him. Ultimately, they did have to remove it.

Jeremy's mom placed the wristband in her son's hand for the visitation. Many friends and relatives asked what it was, and this opened the door for the family to share Jeremy's greatest love—the gospel. Even in this time of sorrow the family could share their hope.

"Always be prepared to give an answer to everyone who asks you to give the reason for the hope that you have. But do this with gentleness and respect."

1 PETER 3:15 (NIV)

Fear Not

Strength   Courage

Deuteronomy 31:6

For the Lord thy God is with thee

This T-shirt was introduced in 2011

Fear Not!

By Tim LaHaye

One of the greatest gifts God has given mankind is His ability to tell us what is coming. In Isaiah 46, He lovingly shows us that only He knows the end from the beginning and that when He purposes in His heart to do something…He does it!

Can there be a greater comfort than that?

Early on in the Bible, we see God's mercy extended in this way, in a famous "fear not" passage. The occasion is the transfer of power after the death of Moses, to his successor, Joshua.

Now, Joshua was a mighty man of great courage. Do you want to know what I think his secret was? He simply believed God. He knew that God's promises were sure and, after all, what is a promise but a confirmation of a future event, as we stand here in the present?

> Be strong and of a good courage; be not afraid, neither be thou dismayed: for the Lᴏʀᴅ thy God is with thee whithersoever thou goest. Joshua 1:9 HJᴜ

In verse nine of Joshua 1 ᴋᴊᴠ, we read: "Be strong and of a good courage; be not afraid, neither be thou dismayed: for the Lᴏʀᴅ thy God is with thee whithersoever thou goest."

I have lived long enough in this world to know beyond a shadow of a doubt that this is true. No matter your circumstances and no matter your age, you can rest assured that because God has given us the gift of fulfilled prophecy, we know that while we might go through rough places for a time, in the end God brings us through.

The declaration, "I will be with you" is the most practical guarantee in all of Scripture, given to Moses, the children of Israel (Deut. 31:6), Joshua, and others, and confirmed by Jesus to Christians through the ages in the Great Commission (Matt. 28:19–20).

My friends, I have studied Bible prophecy for many years, and I have never known God to lie or to be wrong about anything He told us would happen. We are living in a great age of change—not all of it good—but we are also witnessing a moment in which we can put our fears in His hands.

You can read all the self-help books you want. You can listen to all the motivational speakers you have time for—but if you want to find the real key to getting rid of fear, read the mighty prophecies of Scripture and understand how they have been fulfilled to the letter!

TIM LAHAYE pastored for 25 years in San Diego, California, assisted in the founding of the Institute for Creation Research, and has written more than 60 nonfiction books on a wide range of subjects in facing and handling the challenges of life. Tim also coauthored with Jerry B. Jenkins the *Left Behind* fiction series that has broken all publishing records with a total of 80 million in print. LaHaye and his wife, Beverly, have been married for more than 60 years and live in southern California. They have four children, nine grandchildren, and ten great-grandchildren.

BE STRONG

PHILIPPIANS

STRENGTH

4:13

I can do all
things through

Christ who
strengthens me.

Philippians

THINGS

This T-shirt was introduced in 2011

I Can Do All Things through Christ Who Strengthens Me.

Philippians 4:13

By J.C. Watts

I have been in the belly of politics now for more than 20 years. I've also spent time in athletics, business, and ministry. In every one of these areas I've made every effort to get better spiritually but have found it a tougher process in politics. I found that the reason is because everything Scripture encourages us to do in growing spiritually goes against the grain of what politics teaches.

God says, "Turn the other cheek."
Politics says, "That makes you look weak."
God says, "If you want to be first, be last

Politics encourages a "me first" approach. God says, "If you want to receive, give." In politics, folks are usually looking to receive, not give. God says, "Do unto others as you would have them do unto you." Politics says, "Do it to them before they do it to you."

God encourages us to forgive.
Politics says, "No way."

I have some experience with this one. I had left a particular political office, and after two years, Christ had put on my heart to go to a gentleman and beg his forgiveness for how I felt about him. At first I debated God but eventually saw the wisdom in letting go. I did what Christ had put on my heart to do and went to the gentleman and confessed that my heart toward him, when I left that respective office, wasn't Christian.

He told me he understood, and we shook hands. However, several times in the last 10 years this gentleman has resorted to his old tricks of destruction.

One might ask, as I used to ask God, "How can I turn the other cheek?

How can I forgive this guy?"

Well, to be honest with you, when trying to do it on my own, in my flesh or in my strength, I couldn't. But, in times like these, we can turn to Philippians 4:13 (NKJV), which says, "I can do all things through Christ who strengthens me." Making a choice to allow His strength to work through us makes forgiving worth it. So BE STRONG In Christ!

JULIUS CAESAR "J. C." WATTS JR. is a politician from Oklahoma who was a college football quarterback for the Oklahoma Sooners and played professionally in the Canadian Football League. Watts served in the U.S. House of Representatives from 1995 to 2003 as a Republican, representing the 4th Congressional District in south-central Oklahoma. Since leaving Congress he has established a lobbying and consulting firm, serves on corporate boards, and works as a political commentator.

if God has a
fridge your
picture is on it

You are precious
in my eyes...
and I love you.
     —God

Romans 8:16

This Kerusso T-shirt was
introduced in 2012

Precious

BY JANE KIRKPATRICK

Like many of us, my kitchen refrigerator holds the gallery of joy. A paper heart with loving words from the fifth grader I tutor in the English Language Learner program. Photos of family and friends. Postcards sent from travelers enticing us to exotic places around the world. A picture of whomever is president of the United States. Magnets with scriptures written on them help hold everything up. I even have alphabet letters I change often to express hopes and joys for the coming days.

I also have a sign inside my refrigerator written on a Post-it note that reads "It's not in here." Author Geneen Roth, in a book titled *When You Eat in Front of the Refrigerator Pull up a Chair,* suggested such a sign. I've kept one in my fridge for years. Sometimes guests will help me out and open that refrigerator,

The Spirit himself testifies with our spirit that we are God's children.

—Romans 8:16 NIV

read the sign, and ask, "What's not in here?" It's a perfect chance to tell the story. When we're feeling low and insignificant, as humans, we often look for nurture as we did when we were children. The most immediate satisfaction we seek is found in food—or so we think. When I'm feeling inadequate, sad, or lonely, I'll meander toward the refrigerator. I open the door and graze, looking for nurture. Sadly, I will still sometimes settle for potato salad. I can recognize that isn't nurturing at all!

That little sign reminds me that whatever it is I'm looking for to bring me comfort, to remind me that I am precious in God's sight, is not in the food. Nurture is not on that shelf between the leftover green beans or the low-fat yogurt. Nurture is found in filling up with the love God offers.

I have no doubt that if God had a refrigerator, my face—and yours—would be on it because it's where we put our precious photos and sayings. Comfort food isn't inside: it's on the outside where God reaches into our hearts and holds us close. From that relationship, we fill up!

JANE KIRKPATRICK, an award-winning author and speaker, grew up in Wisconsin and earned a master's degree in social work. Eventually, she and her husband, Jerry, decided to homestead in Oregon, and today, they live in Bend. The Kirkpatricks have two children and two grandchildren. Check out Jane's website at www.jkbooks.com.

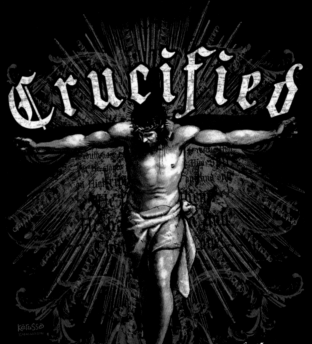

Father, forgive them; for they know not what they do. – Luke 23:34

This T-shirt was introduced in 2008

Pierced for Our Transgressions

By Josh and Sean McDowell

When the great Messianic prophecies were given hundreds of years before Christ's birth, the Roman method of execution—the ghastly crucifixion—was not yet known. Yet in Zechariah 12:10 we read:

"…They pierced my hands and feet."

Jesus was crucified in the usual Roman manner; the hands and feet were pierced by large, dull spikes, which attached the body to the wooden cross or stake.

We have written and spoken many times about the historical evidence for the crucifixion. It happened! This event was ordained by God the Father so that Jesus could pay the penalty for sin, thus restoring the believer to fellowship with his Creator.

Happily though, we know that only days after this cruel death, another prophecy was fulfilled: He is risen!

Some people discount the possibility of the resurrection because it is a miracle. Here are three quick facts that support the claim that Jesus rose from the dead.

FACT 1: Jesus died on the cross. The evidence for Jesus' death by crucifixion is overwhelming. First, there is the fact that all four Gospels report Jesus' death. Second, the nature of the crucifixion virtually guaranteed death. Crucifixion was scientifically honed by the Romans to utterly torture victims. Third, the spear in the side reported by John (ch. 19), in which water and blood recede, is medical evidence that Jesus was dead. Fourth, there is extra-biblical evidence (Tacitus and Josephus) who report that Jesus died by crucifixion.

FACT 2: The tomb of Jesus was found empty on the third day. While there are multiple arguments for the empty tomb, let's consider one of my favorites. Amazingly, the tomb was discovered by women. In Palestine, around the time of Christ, women were not educated or considered reliable sources of information. In fact, Josephus reports that women could not even testify in a court of law. Thus, if the disciples simply fabricated the story of the resurrection, they never would have chosen women to be the first eyewitnesses.

FACT 3: Jesus appeared to people after his death. One of the best evidences for the appearances of Jesus is in 1 Corinthians 15:3–8. Paul recites a creed that can be traced back to within 3–5 years of the death of Jesus. Historically speaking, this is an incredibly early account. Paul records that Jesus appeared to the disciples and also to 500 people.

But why does the resurrection matter? For one thing, Paul says that if Jesus did not resurrect, then our faith is in vain (1 Corinthians 15:14, 17). But the resurrection also shows that God is good, God can be trusted, and that the pain and evil in the world will ultimately be redeemed for good.

JOSH MCDOWELL is perhaps the best-known American apologetics teacher, and a prolific author. As a young man professing to be an atheist, he was challenged to intellectually examine the claims of Christianity… and this led to his faith in Christ. His classic works, *Evidence That Demands a Verdict* and *More Than a Carpenter*, have been read by millions. Josh has spoken to more than 10 million young people, giving over 24,000 talks in 118 countries.

SEAN MCDOWELL is a gifted communicator with a passion for reaching the younger generation with the gospel message. He serves as head of the Bible Department at Capistrano Valley Christian Schools, where he teaches Philosophy, Theology, and Apologetics. A very popular speaker at conferences and an author, he lives in San Juan Capistrano, California, with his wife, Stephanie, and their two children.

No nails held Him to the Cross.
His love for you did!
He could have called on the angels to rescue Him, but He stayed there. They beat Him, spit on Him, ripped His beard out and still
He forgave them.
He has forgiven you.

Kerusso

Back of
Crucified
T-shirt

MY LIFEGUARD

MATTHEW 14:22-32

WALKS ON WATER

This T-shirt was introduced in 2008.

UNSINKABLE!

By Cheri Hamilton

As the morning sun glistened upon the peaceful waters of the offshore reef break, the unthinkable happened, a surfer's worst fear come true! In the blink of an eye our lives were changed forever when a 14.5' tiger shark charged straight up from the deep blue channel along the reef, and in a fraction of a second my 13-year-old daughter's arm was gone, almost to the shoulder. The attack was clean, precise, and over in an instant.

Bethany remembered her training at a lifeguard class for kids, where she had been taught to remain calm in an emergency to prevent excessive blood loss. Clinging to life, Bethany quietly prayed as she lay in the loving hands of the greatest "Lifeguard" one would ever need!

As it was, she lost 60 percent of her blood before reaching the hospital an hour and a half away if you obey the speed limit. Ironically, Bethany's dad, Tom, was already at the hospital being prepped for knee surgery. His operating room became hers as he was wheeled off to a waiting room and temporarily forgotten about, numb from the waist down, unable to move - giving him time alone to pray!

As a mother receiving the early news, I immediately focused on prayer for her life to be spared as I drove too fast to the hospital. I was well aware of the many dangers and repercussions from unclean mouths on sharks, from all the school projects done by her brothers. I also remembered the prayer focus Bethany and I had together, asking God to use her surfing to glorify Him and use it to share His love with the whole world. It was a big prayer, and we didn't expect such a big answer! I thought, "This could be the answer to that prayer, much more than we could ever have imagined, beyond all expectations of answered prayer."

Our heavenly "Lifeguard" was there that morning, watching, guarding, keeping, saving Bethany as she was brought to shore and laid upon the golden sand of one of the most beautiful beaches in the world. That morning, making it to the beach was a series of miracles that took place by the hand of our heavenly Father. His divine protection and rescue was operating in full force. Not only was He saving our daughter, Bethany, but He was about to use her life and love for Him to save others in need of salvation and healing all over the world. As her championship trophies slowly rust and collect dust, lost and lonely lives are being brought into God's glorious kingdom, rescued from eternal death by our greatest Lifeguard, Jesus Christ.

Today Bethany is following her dream of being a professional surfer. But more importantly, she is representing Jesus with all of her heart, mind and soul.

"OUR HEAVENLY 'LIFEGUARD' WAS THERE THAT MORNING, WATCHING, GUARDING, KEEPING, SAVING BETHANY..."

CHERI HAMILTON is the mother of Bethany Hamilton and lives with her husband Tom in Hawaii. In 2007, a documentary, *Heart of a Soul Surfer*, was made, detailing the family's ordeal and achieving international acclaim. In 2011 *Soul Surfer*, a major motion picture, was produced based on Bethany's life story along with *Raising a Soul Surfer*, a book written by Cheri Hamilton revealing the amazing details of Bethany's story and the hand of God upon their family.

COURAGEOUS

HONOR BEGINS AT HOME

I WILL BE

COURAGEOUS

JOSHUA 24:15

LOVE · SERVE · PROTECT

AS FOR ME AND MY HOUSE,

WE WILL SERVE THE LORD.

Honor Begins at Home

Kerusso

Courageous title treatment and images used by arrangement with Sherwood Pictures/Provident Film.

COURAGEOUS
HONOR BEGINS AT HOME

This T-shirt was introduced in 2011.

GOOD COURAGE, GOOD DADS

BY ALEX AND STEPHEN KENDRICK

How did two pastor-brothers from Georgia find themselves making films? The obvious answer is that the Lord brought it about, of course.

He also mercifully gave the staff of Sherwood Pictures—a ministry of Sherwood Baptist Church in Albany, Georgia, where we are associate pastors—a bit of the courage that He imparted to Joshua.

The example of the biblical battler of giants has helped us produce independent films like *Facing the Giants*, *Fireproof*, and *Courageous*. Our first film, made a decade ago, was *Flywheel*.

"Courageous" is a film that resonates strongly in our culture today and is based on Joshua 24:15— *"Choose today who you will serve, but as for me and my house, we will serve the Lord."*

What the Lord tends to do every time we go through that season of prayer before we decide what the movie's going to be about…is that the Lord always gives a story that to some extent is going to be about self-surgery. With fatherhood, we realized just how crucial our role is.

The line in the film,

"It's not okay just to be a 'good-enough dad,'"
came after our research and a realization that we were just "good-enough" dads—and that's not good enough!

We have to be very intentional about calling our daughters to womanhood, and our sons to manhood.

The plot of the film—a local police force battling a drug ring—is enhanced by the interaction of the individual officers who have major repairs to make with their own families.

It takes courage for fathers today just to get through the daily list of responsibilities. Yet what we see modeled in *Courageous* requires taking an extra step. The biblical concept of fatherhood comes from our heavenly Father, who tells us repeatedly that He will never leave us. In our broken world, that is an example that is desperately needed in all families, no matter their backgrounds.

Alex and Stephen Kendrick, natives of Georgia, are the writing/directing/producing team behind Sherwood Pictures, a ministry outreach of Sherwood Baptist Church in Albany, Georgia.

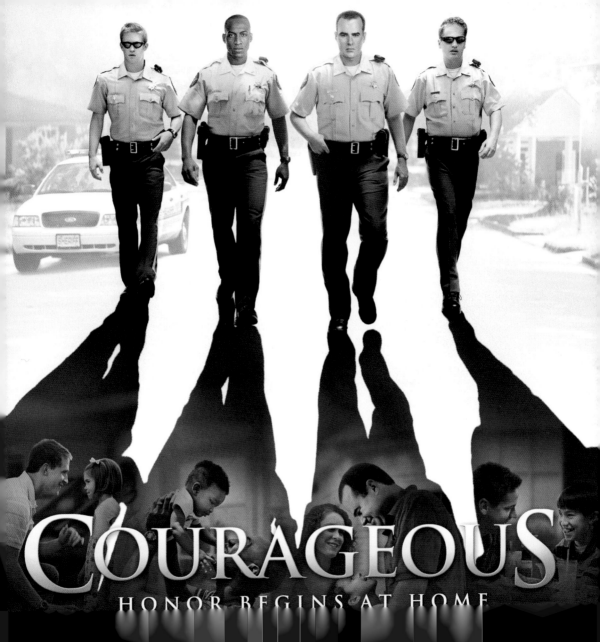

DANCE
SING
PRAISE
LIVE
LOVE

AS LONG AS I LIVE
I WILL SING & PRAISE
THE LORD GOD
Psalm 104

This T-shirt was introduced in 2012.

STILL PRAISING HIM

by TAMMY TRENT

I knew when I was six years old and playing the drums for the first time that making music was going to be a big part of my life's journey. From the beginning, it seems my life has been about the beauty of worshipping God somehow through it all—to dance, sing, praise, and live and love big, no matter what life threw at me.

My mom had a profound influence on me through her own ministry of music and teaching. It seemed natural that I would one day follow that same path, performing Christian music of my own. But I certainly learned early on that this was much bigger than me and had nothing to do with building a career. It had everything to do with building a ministry that would prayerfully change a life, including mine. And so that journey began in 1995 when I signed my first record deal.

Psalm 104:33 is one of my favorites, as it truly sums up my heart. I long to use my voice to help others find a true, authentic relationship with Jesus and to fully understand His promises and deep commitment to us, especially when we feel all alone. I look at this open door in my life with a faithful heart, and I thank God for trusting me with it.

As you can see, I'm pretty passionate about the things of God, living life to the fullest, and trying to help others see that potential too. As I travel and speak and sing (including with Women of Faith and Revolve), I realize that I've been given such an amazing opportunity to minister and share my life and my hope with others. It has been a life that has faced a deep, tragic loss in September 2001 and left me a young widow. But it is the hope of Christ that has brought me back to my feet again, praising God for carrying me one more day! And I believe He will do the same for you if you'll let Him.

Acts 1:8 is also very meaningful to me, as I cherish the Holy Spirit's power in my life daily and testify for Him.

Life is a gift from God, and there's nothing we cannot do or accomplish without His strength! Walk in great purpose, passion, and power in your life in Jesus's name! You've got this!

TAMMY TRENT Beneath her youthful exterior and fresh-faced exuberance, Tammy is a focused recording artist, author, and speaker who knows exactly what she wants to say. She creates music that serves as a personal conduit for those seeking to worship God and also wants to remind others of God's desire to reach them. Through her own personal journey of love and loss, Tammy continues to share that theme through her books, her music, and her life. www.tammytrent.com

AS LONG AS I LIVE,

I WILL SING & PRAISE

THE LORD GOD.

HOW DO WE LIVE FOR HIM?

It was surely the ugliest argument in the history of God's kingdom.

Jesus had invested three years, teaching His disciples God's values and priorities. They had just witnessed Moses and Elijah speaking to Jesus on the Mount of Transfiguration, and a question arose: Did that mean that Moses and Elijah were the most important in all of heaven? Then the debate heated up and got personal: Which one of *them*, Jesus's disciples, was the most important? Knowing that this was what they were arguing about, Jesus's heart was so broken, He couldn't bring Himself to even walk with them on the road to Capernaum. The cross was one week away. We don't know what each disciple said to make the case for his own importance, but surely it was who could most impressively "live for Him"—who could do the most, the biggest, the best for Jesus and His kingdom.

Later that evening, He answered their who-is-the-greatest argument by placing a child in front of them: "It is the one who is least among you all who is the greatest" (Luke 9:48 NIV). "Unless you change and become like little children, you

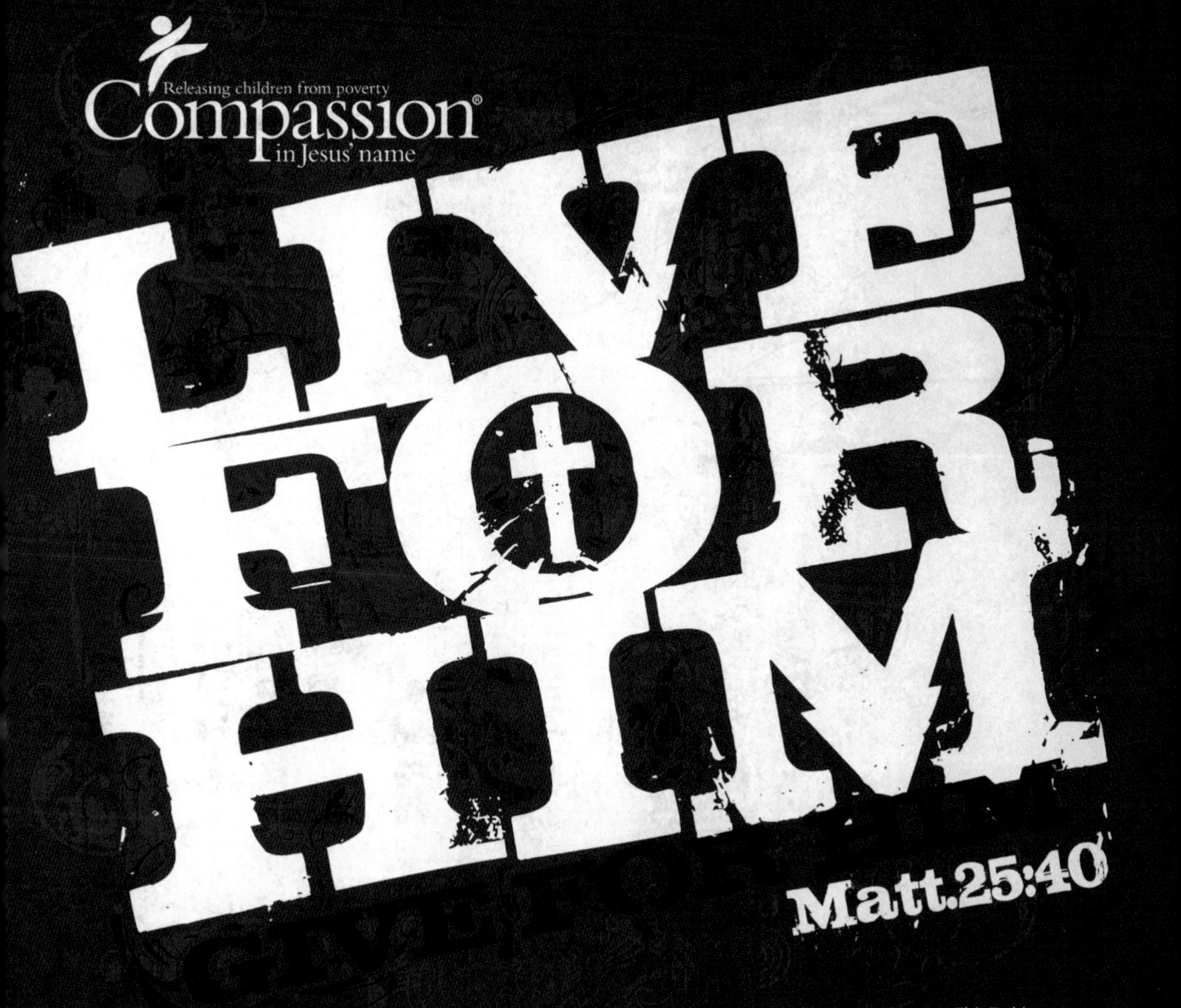

LIVE FOR HIM

Matt. 25:40

This T-shirt was
produced from 2009
to 2011

will never enter [*much less be a leader in*] the kingdom of heaven" (Matt. 18:3 NIV). He admonished them to stop being so child*ish* and challenged them instead to become more child*like*. He told them how to live for Him: "Whoever welcomes this little child in my name welcomes me" (Luke 9:48 NIV). And He said it even more clearly in Matthew 25:40 NIV: "Whatever you do for one of the least of these … you did for me." *Want to serve Me? Serve them. Want to give to Me? Give to them. Want to live for Me? Live for them!* "Speak up for those who cannot speak for themselves" (Prov. 31:8 NIV)!

For nearly its entire twenty-five-year history, Kerusso has partnered with Compassion International. Our joint hallmark has been caring for "the least of these." If you have supported Kerusso over these years, you have blessed children—and wonderfully, mysteriously, you have "lived for Him."

DR. WESS STAFFORD is president of Compassion International, an internationally recognized advocate for children in poverty. His daily radio feature, "Speak Up With Compassion" is heard on over 800 radio stations in the United States.

He earned degrees from Moody Bible Institute, Wheaton, and a PhD from Michigan State University. Wess lives on a small ranch near Colorado Springs, Colorado, with his wife, Donna, of 32 years, who was a Compassion sponsor even before she met Wess! They have two daughters, Jenny and Katie—the two children in the world for whom Wess is the greatest advocate of all.

...I TELL YOU THE TRUTH, WHEN YOU DID IT TO ONE OF THE LEAST OF THESE MY BROTHERS AND SISTERS, YOU WERE DOING IT TO ME

— *Jesus*

Back of *Live for Him* T-shirt

PARTING
THOUGHTS

I HOPE YOU ENJOYED THIS LITTLE BOOK, MY LABOR OF LOVE.

I hope you enjoyed reading about a kid who went from atheist to follower of Jesus Christ and on to become a worldwide preacher of the gospel.

If you are already a T-shirt Evangelist, I pray that this book and the testimonies of fellow believers have deepened your resolve to continue sharing our faith with the world. The time is short.

If you're a believer but have never tried fulfilling the Great Commission in a specific and personal way, I hope this book has inspired you to try T-shirt evangelism as a way to do that. I know it will be a rewarding and fulfilling experience.

I hope you were edified by the wonderful devotions contributed at no cost by my artist and author friends. Please look into their most recent and upcoming works as the Lord leads.

If you are not yet a believer, I hope this book and my personal story are causing you to rethink that position.

What's holding you back? For me it was false "knowledge." I believed the lie the world and the devil have been telling us for centuries: "There is no God." Friends, I'm here to tell you that the mountain of evidence points in exactly the opposite direction.

If you feel uneasy about your current belief that He isn't real or isn't worth serving, then I urge you to investigate my claims more deeply. You have nothing to lose—and everything to gain.

If God is speaking to you in your heart and you're ready to answer Him right now, then pray this prayer to God. Be reborn to a new life in Him;

God, I feel You calling me and I want to be Your child.

I've changed my thinking about some things, and You are changing my heart.

I want You more than I want my way or my sins.

God, Your Word says in Romans 10:9 that if I declare with my mouth, "Jesus is Lord," and believe in my heart that You raised him from the dead, then I will be saved.

So God, right now I declare out loud that Jesus is Lord! He is Lord of the universe and Lord of my life from now on! God, I believe in my heart that You raised Jesus from the dead after He paid for my sins by dying on the cross. From this moment on I know that I am saved, because Your Word is true! No matter what—I will hold fast to my confession of faith in You! You are now my Father, and I am now Your child. I know that You love me with all Your heart, and nothing can ever change that.

In Jesus' Name, amen.

Praise God! Congratulations! You have made the most important decision of your life. Now go and grow in the knowledge of Him. Start reading the Bible, beginning with the New Testament. Go to someone you respect that you know to be an honorable believer and tell them about your new life in Jesus. Find a good Christian radio station and listen as you can. There are many anointed preachers of the Word of God who will build you up in your new faith. Find a Bible believing and preaching church to attend. We weren't meant to go this new life alone. You have new brothers and sisters to meet who will help you in your walk with Jesus!

Thank you all so much for purchasing and reading this book.

If you liked it, please recommend it to your friends and loved ones.

Don't be strangers! Please e-mail and share your T-shirt Evangelism stories with us. We feed on good words from the field.

Also, let me know if you prayed that prayer above and began your new life in Christ. I want to rejoice with you!

GOD BLESS YOU, MY FRIENDS!

Vic

Email me:
Share@kerusso.com

Write us:
Kerusso
Attn: Vic Kennett
402 HWY 62 Spur
Berryville, AR 72616

Join us:
facebook.com/kerussoshirts

How can they believe in Him if they
have never heard about Him?

And how can they hear about Him
unless someone tells them?

From Romans 10:14

Change Your Shirt.
Change The World!